FREGE'S THEORY
OF JUDGEMENT

FREGE'S THEORY
OF JUDGEMENT

BY
DAVID BELL

CLARENDON PRESS · OXFORD
1979

Oxford University Press, Walton Street, Oxford OX2 6DP

OXFORD   LONDON   GLASGOW
NEW YORK   TORONTO   MELBOURNE   WELLINGTON
KUALA LUMPUR   SINGAPORE   JAKARTA   HONG KONG   TOKYO
DELHI   BOMBAY   CALCUTTA   MADRAS   KARACHI
NAIROBI   DAR ES SALAAM   CAPE TOWN

Published in the United States by
Oxford University Press, New York

British Library Cataloguing in Publication Data

Bell, David Andrew
    Frege's theory of judgement.
    1. Frege, Gottlob—Knowledge, Theory of
    2. Judgement
    I. Title
    121   B3245.F24   79-40387

    ISBN 0-19-827423-8

Printed in Great Britain
by W & J Mackay Limited, Chatham

for

LAURA

PREFACE

In order to reduce the number of footnotes to a minimum—though there are still far too many of them—I have incorporated as many references as possible into the text. All unqualified numerical references are to page numbers (with the sole exception of references to Wittgenstein's *Tractatus*, which are by '*Satz*' number, as is conventional); and all page numbers are those of the original edition or publication of the work in question. Many of Frege's articles originally appeared in periodicals and journals not now easily available; but this creates no problem as virtually all German reprints and English translations indicate the original pagination.

Reliable translations into English exist of most of the German works quoted herein and, within only occasional modification, I have employed these where available. In those cases (most notably Frege's correspondence and *Nachlass*) where no published English translation exists, I have translated the German myself.

I am indebted to McMaster University for financial support while in Hamilton, and to the Deutscher Akademischer Austauschdienst for enabling me to pursue my research in Göttingen and Konstanz. To Mr. Kenneth Blackwell of the Bertrand Russell Archives at McMaster University, and to Herrn Albert Veraart, Dr. Gottfried Gabriel, and the Frege-Archiv at Konstanz, go my sincere thanks for their always friendly co-operation and helpful advice. Professor G.-H. Gadamer has been kind enough to check some of my translations from the German.

Most of all, however, I am indebted to Professors Peter Nidditch, Günther Patzig, Michael Resnik, and Neil Wilson, who have, in reading either the present or earlier versions of this work, provided helpful advice, often forceful criticism, and much valuable encouragement.

Much of the final draft of the book was written in St. Margaret's Hope, Orkney; for doing so much to provide what were virtually ideal conditions in which to write, my sincere thanks go to O.H., L.H., and L.D.

Sheffield
April 1978

CONTENTS

LIST OF ABBREVIATIONS

A.   *Critique of Pure Reason*, 1st edition, 1781, (Kant)
ASB.   'Ausführungen über Sinn und Bedeutung'. (Frege)
B.   *Critique of Pure Reason*, 2nd edition, 1787. (Kant)
Brief.   *Wissenschaftlicher Briefwechsel.* (Frege)
Bs.   *Begriffsschrift . . . etc.* (Frege)
BuG.   'Über Begriff und Gegenstand'. (Frege)
FPL.   *Frege: Philosophy of Language.* (Dummett)
FuB.   *Funktion und Begriff.* (Frege)
Funk.   'Was ist eine Funktion?' (Frege)
G&B.   *Translations from . . . Frege.* (Ed. P. T. Geach, M. Black)
Ged.   'Der Gedanke'. (Frege)
Gef.   'Gedankengefüge'. (Frege)
Gg.   *Grundgesetze der Arithmetik.* (Frege)
Gl.   *Die Grundlagen der Arithmetik.* (Frege)
KBS.   'Kritische Beleuchtung . . . E. Schröders . . . etc.' (Frege)
Klemke   *Essays on Frege.* (Ed. E. D. Klemke)
Nach.   *Nachgelassene Schriften.* (Frege)
NB.   *Notebooks, 1914–1916.* (Wittgenstein)
PG.   *Philosophical Grammar.* (Wittgenstein)
PI.   *Philosophical Investigations.* (Wittgenstein)
PMs.   *The Principles of Mathematics.* (Russell)
SuB.   'Über Sinn und Bedeutung'. (Frege)
TLP.   *Tractatus Logico-Philosophicus.* (Wittgenstein)
Vern.   'Verneinung'. (Frege)

Further details of these works may be found in the Bibliography.

ASP: Archiv für systematische Philosophie.
BPI: Beiträge zur Philosophie des deutschen Idealismus.
*BVK: Berichte über die Verhandlungen der Königlich Sächsischen
     Gesellschaft der Wissenschaften zu Leipzig.*
J. of Phil.: The Journal of Philosophy.
PAS: Proceedings of the Aristotelian Society.
PAS (Supp.): Proceedings of the Aristotelian Society, Supplementary
     series.
Ph. of Sc.: Philosophy of Science.
Philos.: Philosophy.
Phil. Rev.: The Philosophical Review.

Phil. Studs.: Philosophical Studies.
QJPAM.: The Quarterly Journal of Pure and Applied Mathematics.
Rev. Met.: The Review of Metaphysics.
VWP:　Vierteljahrsschrift für wissenschaftliche Philosophie.
ZPK: Zeitschrift für Philosophie und philosophische Kritik.

INTRODUCTION

1. SINCE the beginning of the present century the notion of a 'theory of judgement' has fallen, if not into actual disrepute, then at least into desuetude. Certainly it no longer occupies the position of pre-eminence it once enjoyed in the works of Bradley, Moore, or Russell, say, or those of the classical German idealists. The reasons for this neglect are not, I think, hard to discover. In the first place, in post-Kantian philosophy the theory of judgement was all too often handmaiden to a monolithic, revisionary, and often idealist meta-physical system. Judgement, it was urged, is the primordial act in terms of which we make sense of the world. But all too frequently in the account given of judgement no possibility was allowed of its making contact with reality as it is in itself, independently of the judgements we formulate about it. And so judgement became not merely the act by means of which we make sense of the world, but, in a much stronger sense, the means by which we 'constitute' or 'con-struct' a world. The tenor of twentieth-century philosophy has, on the whole, been antithetical to such idealist metaphysical systems, and the theory of judgement has suffered neglect partly as a result of being associated with them.

A second, more important reason for this neglect lies in the fact that many of the legitimate functions performed by the erstwhile theory of judgement have, since the beginning of this century, increasingly been performed by 'the theory of meaning'—a central part of the philosophy of language. Thus the philosophical examina-tion of notions once central to the theory of judgement, notions such as *concept*, *thought*, *judgement*, *meaning*, and *truth*, has come to be conducted by employing their linguistic analogues as a model. Frege was explicit about this: '. . . even a thought grasped by a human being for the very first time can be put in a form of words which will be understood by someone to whom the thought is entirely new. This would be impossible were we not able to distinguish parts in the thought corresponding to the parts in the sentence, so that the structure of the sentence serves as a model for the structure of the thought.' (*Gef*.36.) The theory of judgement has thus been displaced from the centre of the philosophical stage in favour of concerns more overtly linguistic; but many of the aims, doctrines, concepts, and problems central to the former remain essentially unchanged beneath their new linguistic guise. It is no accident that amongst the concepts fundamental to Frege's *semantic* theory are those of *concept, thought, assertion, sense,* and *truth*—concepts which bear more than a passing resemblance to those, mentioned above, which were central to the traditional theory of judgement.

A third reason for the current neglect of the theory of judgement lies in the massive changes which, mainly as a result of Frege's work, the whole discipline of logic has this century undergone. In the past, philosophers and logicians as diverse as Aristotle, William of Occam, Kant, Hegel, Lotze, and W. S. Jevons have adopted what was, prima facie at least, an intuitively attractive way of classifying the central issues in logic. Logic, that is, was typically divided into three parts, which, in ascending order, were:

1. the doctrine of terms,
2. the doctrine of propositions,
3. the doctrine of syllogisms.

Now there is, indeed, nothing philosophically pernicious in this system of classification—at least so long as it is not taken to reflect some underlying ontological or epistemological reality. Unfortunately, it often was just so taken. The elements which comprise a proposition are terms, the elements which comprise an argument are propositions; and just as one cannot understand an argument without first understanding the propositions of which it is composed, so (the argument ran) one cannot understand a proposition without first understanding the terms of which it is composed. In studying logic, then, one inevitably begins with the doctrine of terms and only when this has been formulated is one in a position to proceed to an examination of the nature of propositions. Theories of this sort are not easily able to account for what truth there is in the claim that what a term means is what it contributes to the meaning of propositions in which it occurs. But worse was to come. To this ordered logico-linguistic trichotomy, it was maintained, there corresponds an exactly parallel division of the human discursive faculties. The following passage is a typical statement of what was widely taken to be a quite uncontroversial doctrine: 'If when reduced to language there be three parts of logic, terms, propositions, and syllogisms, there must be as many different kinds of thought or operations of the mind. These are usually called—

1. Simple apprehension
2. Judgement
3. Reasoning . . .'.[1]

And judgement, the author adds, 'consists in comparing together two notions or ideas . . . derived from simple apprehension'. Traditionally, then, the theory of judgement was that 'second part' of epistemology which dealt with human propositional abilities. And a judgement was assumed to be a complex whole constructed out of the independently significant elements provided by simple apprehension; elements known variously as 'ideas', 'notions', 'impressions', 'sensations', or 'concepts'.

Two questions suggest themselves at this point: one concerns the *origin* of our ideas; the other, the *objectivity* of our judgements. If ideas are mental entities, existing only in or for consciousness, and if judgements are comprised of such ideas, then the act of judgement is in danger of turning out to be a solipsistic act. How, then, are we able to judge about the world, and not merely about our ideas? And whence these ideas anyway? The same answer is typically provided to both these questions in theories of this kind; for, it is claimed, it is the origin of (at least some of) our ideas which accounts for the objectivity of (at least some of) our judgements. Our contact with objective reality is sensory, and it is in this contact that ideas originate. Simple apprehension is, then, a sensory phenomenon, and the link with objective reality which it represents is preserved, so it is maintained, when ideas are subsequently employed as the elements in a judgement.

There are a number of defects which seem to be endemic to such accounts of the nature of judgement. In the first place, for example, there is the virtually inevitable assimilation of the sensory to the intellectual. If the origin of our ideas lies in our sensory contact with reality, and if a judgement is a complex whose parts are such ideas, then it would seem that sensations and judgements differ not at all in kind but only in degree; that there is, in other words, a 'sensory/intellectual continuum'. But the claim that an itch is the same sort of thing as the judgement that $2+3=5$, for example, differing from it

---

[1] W. S. Jevons, *Elementary Lessons in Logic*, London, 1875, p. 11.

only in degree (of complexity, or vivacity, or clarity, or distinctness, or whatever), is so entirely implausible that avoidance of any commitment to it can only be regarded as a virtue in a theory of judgement.[2]

A second difficulty endemic to such theories of judgement is their inability to account for the *unity* of judgement and thought. If judgements are built up out of pre-existent and independently significant elements, then we need an explanation of why a judgement is not merely a list, or string, or sequence of such elements: 'But the question now arises how the thought comes to be constructed, and how its parts so combine together that the whole amounts to something more than the parts taken separately.' (*Gef.*36.) The judgement that Simone Martini did not decorate Wigan town hall, for example, possesses a unity, a completeness, an internal coherence which is entirely absent from the mere string of ideas, of Simone Martini, Wigan, town hall, negation, decoration ... and so on. An explanation of this fundamental phenomenon is not forthcoming under the traditional theory. (This problem is taken up again in section 3, below.)

The present work primarily concerns Frege's theory of judgement —though frequent reference is also made to the works of Kant and Wittgenstein. Now these three philosophers have at least this in common: they agree in rejecting in its entirety one of the main presuppositions of traditional theories of judgement. They reject, that is, the claim that ideation or conception may precede, or occur independently of judgement, and, hence, that judgement can be adequately analysed as the putting together of independently significant elements. Frege stated this explicitly in a letter of May 1882 (written either to Marty or to Stumpf): 'Now I don't believe that the formation of concepts can precede judgement, because that presupposes that concepts can exist independently; rather, I think that concepts emerge from the breaking up of a possible content of judgement.' (*Brief.*164. Cf.*Nach.*18.) In a remarkably similar passage, in *Die falsche Spitzfindigkeit der vier syllogistischen Figuren*, Kant had written: 'It is clear that in the ordinary treatment of logic there is serious error, in that distinct and complete concepts are treated before judgements and ratiocinations, although the former are only possible by means of the latter.' Concepts, that is, can lead no independent life outside the context of human judgements: 'The *only* use

---

[2] A detailed examination of this continuum hypothesis is contained in J. Bennett's *Kant's Dialectic*, Cambridge, 1974, §§4–6.

which the understanding can make of . . . concepts is to judge by means of them.' (*B*.93, my italics.) The linguistic counterpart of this epistemological thesis of the priority of judgements to concepts, is expressed in Frege's famous *Grundlagen* principle that 'Only in the context of a proposition does a word have meaning' (*Gl*.73), a principle to which Wittgenstein subscribed both in the *Tractatus* (*TLP*.3.3) and in the *Investigations* (*PI*.24).

The thesis of the priority of judgements to concepts (and of sentence meaning to word meaning) is, then, a direct denial of the traditional ascending tripartite classification of human discursive faculties (and of logic itself). But this denial creates problems of its own. At the very least we must reconcile the claim that judgements are prior to concepts with the fact that judgements *are*, in some sense, formulated by bringing together already familiar concepts. This tension is even more apparent in the analogous linguistic case: the claim that a word only has meaning in the context of a proposition must be reconciled with the incontestable fact that it is through a prior understanding of the words of which they are composed that we understand sentences which we have not previously encountered. This tension is neatly caught in the following passage from the *Tractatus*:

The meanings of primitive signs can be explained by means of elucidations. Elucidations are propositions that contain the primitive signs. So they can only be understood if the meanings of those signs are *already* known. (*TLP*. 3.263, my italics.)

The resolution of this tension is one of the major tasks which confronts those who would defend a Kantian/Fregean theory of judgement.

2. I suggested above that contemporary analytical philosophers have, on the whole, shown little interest in the theory of judgement. The large number of articles which have appeared during the last thirty years concerning what, following Church, has come to be called 'the analysis of statements of assertion and belief' might, however, seem to constitute an exception to this generalization. The philosophers with whom one associates this activity are, for example, Russell, Carnap, Quine, Church, and Hintikka. And the problem to which they have addressed themselves is that of providing an adequate semantics for a class of sentences which are, paradigmatically, of the form:

(S) $A \phi$'s that p.

Here 'A' is to be replaced by the proper name of a person (or by a definite description or personal pronoun); 'ϕ' is to be replaced by a verb such as 'doubt', 'think', 'judge', 'hope', or 'assert'; and 'p' by any sentence. This will yield a sentence such as:

(1)   John believes that all hope is lost.

The schema (S) represents the form of statements typically used (we are told) to ascribe a belief, judgement, doubt, hope, etc. to a person.

   Now it is not my intention to deny that such sentences as (1) present the linguist, the logician, and the linguistic philosopher with problems and perplexities: on the contrary, I believe that such problems exist, and that they are both intriguing and important. My point is rather to explain why I have not concerned myself with such matters in what follows, as this omission may well surprise those who believe that the analysis of statements of assertion and belief is the only legitimate heir to the activities once encompassed under the notion, now somewhat anachronistic, of a 'theory of judgement'.

   There are, I believe, basically two considerations which together have led philosophers to place so much emphasis upon the analysis of statements of the form (S). The first has been expressed with admirable terseness by Wittgenstein in the *Tractatus*:

In the general propositional form propositions occur in other propositions only as the bases of truth-operations.

At first sight it looks as though it were also possible for one proposition to occur in another in a different way.

Particularly with certain forms of proposition in psychology, such as 'A believes that p is the case' and 'A has the thought that p', etc. (*TLP*.5.54f.)

Wittgenstein's thought here is that while, on the one hand, in a truth-functional proposition such as 'If p then q' or 'p and q, but not-r', the truth-value of the whole is determined by the truth-values of the component propositions (a fact that is manifest in the conventional procedure of laying out the truth conditions in a truth-table), on the other hand, the truth value of (1) in no way depends upon the truth or falsity of the proposition which John believes or thinks. The proposition 'p', as it occurs in the complex 'A believes that p', behaves in a way which presents those who, like Carnap and Wittgenstein, would incline towards a purely extensional semantics with the gravest problems.

But if Wittgenstein and Carnap have interested contemporary philosophers in the purely semantic problems raised by the existence of statements of the form (S), the later Wittgenstein and such philosophers as Austin and Grice have been construed as providing another motive for our taking a closer look at *statements* of belief: they tell us a great deal about the *phenomenon* of belief. Now this is not the place for an examination of the fundamental methodological tenets of analytical or linguistic philosophy; though it is hardly contentious to claim that such philosophy typically proceeds to investigate a given phenomenon by examining the language, or linguistic behaviour, typically associated with it. 'Essence is expressed by grammar,' wrote Wittgenstein, 'Grammar tells us what kind of object anything is.' (*PI*.116.) If the phenomenon under investigation is the nature of judgement, say, then the philosopher might proceed by asking such questions as: What are the typical means by which we ascribe a judgement to others and/or ourselves; and what are our criteria for so doing? What is the logical form of expressions of judgement? And so on. The answers provided to questions of this sort by contemporary analytical philosophers have concerned, almost exclusively, expressions of the form (S). And this, I believe, is a mistake. The paradigmatic form for the expression of a judgement or belief that *p* is the case is not a sentence of the form '*A* ϕ's that *p*', but rather one of the form: '*p*'. To pass a judgement or to express it, and to report or ascribe a judgement are not one and the same activity, any more than to make a promise is the same thing as to report the making of a promise. Statements of the form (S) are primarily relevant to the ascription of judgements, to talk *about* judgements, and not to the formulation, assertion, and expression of judgements. The philosophers with whom this book is primarily concerned—Frege, Kant, and Wittgenstein—have appreciated that it is to direct discourse, and not to oratio obliqua, that one must look for the key to the nature of human judgement. In a sense, a theory of judgement *is* a theory of the proposition; and while such a theory must, of course, accommodate the sub-class of propositions which are of the form (S), it ought not to be based solely upon it.

3. The philosophical problem which forms the background to, though not always the explicit subject-matter of the present investigation

made its first appearance in Plato's *Sophist*, where at one point
the Stranger asserts: 'the question at issue is whether all names may
be connected with one another, or none, or only some of them'.[3] To
this Theaetetus replies that, clearly, the latter is the case. The
Stranger's retort is that it is not only names or nouns, but verbs too,
which are necessary if discourse it to be possible. But even granted
this, he goes on, still not all combinations of nouns and verbs are
meaningful: '[a speaker] not only names, but he does something *by
connecting verbs with nouns*; and therefore we say that he discourses.
. . . And as there are certain things which fit one another, and other
things which do not fit, so there are some vocal signs which do, and
other things which do not combine to form discourse.'[4] In other
words, while

She it in from hid garden the him

is just a *list* or string of eight English words,

She hid it from him in the garden

is a *sentence* which says, or can be used to say, something. In Plato's
metaphor, the words in the sentence 'fit' one another, and so 'combine' to form a whole, a unity; the words in the list, on the other
hand, remain just isolated words.

It is not only in the realm of words, however, that this phenomenon
manifests itself; for just as a sentence possesses a unity quite absent
from a mere list of words, so a thought (or judgement, or proposition)
possesses a unity and completeness entirely absent from a mere
medley or succession of images, impressions, ideas, concepts, or
meanings. For the Ancients this phenomenon was closely related to
the problem of the One and the Many; Wittgenstein dubbed it 'the
essence of the propositional *bond*';[5] Kant, 'the synthetic unity of the
manifold in [representations] in general';[6] and Russell wrote about it
as follows:

A proposition has a certain indefinable unity, in virtue of which it is an
assertion; and this unity is so completely lost by analysis that no enumeration of constituents will restore it, even though itself be mentioned as a
constituent. There is, it must be confessed, a grave logical difficulty in this
fact, for it is difficult not to believe that a whole must be constituted by its
constituents. (*PMs*.466–7.)

---

[3] Plato's *Sophist*, trans. B. Jowett, *The Dialogues of Plato*, vol. iii, p. 530.
[4] Ibid., p. 531, my italics.   [5] *TLP*.4.221. See also *NB*.5, 37, 41.   [6] *B*.105.

And Frege, too, was clearly grappling with the same problem in the following passage from 'Über Begriff und Gegenstand':

... not all the parts of a thought can be complete; at least one must be 'unsaturated' or predicative; otherwise they would not hold together. For example, the sense of the phrase 'the number 2' does not hold together with that of the expression 'the concept *prime number*' without a link. We apply such a link in the sentence
       The number 2 falls under the concept *prime number*;
it is contained in the words 'falls under', which need to be completed in two ways—by a subject and an accusative; and only because their sense is thus unsaturated are they capable of serving as a link. Only when they have been supplemented in this twofold respect do we get a complete sense, a *thought*. (*BuG*.205.)

But it is not only in connection with words and sentences, and with concepts and thoughts that this unity manifests itself. Taking up Frege's (and Plato's) metaphor of 'linking' and 'fitting', Wittgenstein asserted that 'in a state of affairs the objects fit into one another like the links of a chain' (*TLP*.2.03). There seem, in other words, to be three aspects to this phenomenon of propositional unity (as we can call it for the moment): there is the unity of sentences (linguistic), of thoughts and judgements (epistemological), and of states of affairs and facts (ontological). Now plainly these three aspects are very closely related one to another. If, following Russell, Frege, and Wittgenstein, we identify the meaning of a sentence with the thought which it expresses *and* with the state of affairs which it asserts to exist, then the linguistic, epistemological, and ontological aspects merge with one another inextricably. But even if we do not subscribe to any such theory, still it is arguable in general that whatever it is that makes Caesar's loving Cleopatra a complete state of affairs, is so closely related to whatever it is which makes 'Caesar loves Cleopatra' a complete sentence, and to whatever it is that makes the thought that Caesar loves Cleopatra complete, that any explanatory appeal from one to the other must run the gravest risk of bankruptcy. If, as I believe, the linguistic, the epistemological, and the ontological aspects are, indeed, but three different aspects of one and the same fundamental phenomenon, then no complete account of this phenomenon can be expected from within any one of these fields. The solution to the problem of the nature of the 'propositional bond' must needs be a metaphysical solution. But *metaphysical* does not mean *metaphorical*; and some way must be found of translating all the talk of 'bonds', 'chains', 'saturation', 'fitting', 'bundles', 'glue', and 'synthesis' with which literature on this topic has abounded since Plato's time.

The present work does not claim to have offered any final and definitive account of the nature of propositional unity. It is, however, hoped that some light has been thrown on the problem, that some of the metaphors have been translated into more prosaic language, and that, programmatic though it may be, a possible solution has been at least adumbrated.

4. This work is also an extended attempt to answer the question: What is a judgement? And, roughly speaking, the answer will turn out to be that a judgement, at least in the simplest of cases, is an assertion that a given object falls under a particular concept. This, of course, is hardly illuminating until it be established what is an *assertion*, an *object*, a *concept*, and what is the nature of the relation of *falling under*. A philosophical analysis of these concepts will comprise what we might call the logical topography of judgement. What follows is an essay in logical topography in this sense.

5. As though to remind himself that the mental activities of judging and thinking are neither rare nor occult, Wittgenstein wrote: 'Thought *can* only be something common-or-garden, and *ordinary*.' (*PG*.108.) Thinking, that is, is a mundane activity manifested by the vast majority of mankind during the greater part of their waking lives. The nature of judgement and thought is also, prima facie, a problem with which, of all the philosophical disciplines, *epistemology* should deal. A word must be said here, therefore, about my use in the sequel of a series of rather esoteric logical symbols, and, indeed, about my having chosen to concentrate upon Frege—a philosopher with whom one does not immediately associate a concern for matters epistemological. Rulon Wells has summarized the contributions upon which Frege's reputation rests as follows: 'We remember Gottlob Frege (1845–1925) for three primary contributions. He made proof in mathematics and logic more precise and airtight, he showed how the basic notions of logic and mathematics could be assimilated to each other, and he produced a workable philosophy of mathematics.'[7] Now as a historical generalization, this may well be correct. But throughout his career and especially in his later writings Frege was

---

[7] R. S. Wells, 'Frege's Ontology', *Rev. Met.* iv (1951), 537.

also concerned to produce a theory of discursive mental activity which deserves, what it has not yet received, the close attention of philosophers. That Frege's concern was prompted by his logico-mathematical investigations, and that he employed tools developed there to solve problems that are essentially epistemological, should not be allowed to detract from the value of his contribution to the latter subject.

As to the matter of Frege's logical symbolism: much of what follows is devoted precisely to showing why it constitutes a valuable adjunct to a theory of judgement. A few preliminary remarks, however, are here in order. Let us, then, examine briefly the complex sign:

(2) $\vdash\!\!\!-\!\!\!-\!\!\!-\varDelta$

which is the basic form of all complete signs which may occur in the derivations and proofs of Frege's concept-script.[8] This sign has three components. First there is the *functional sign*, concept-word, or predicate:

(3) $-\!\!\!-\!\!\!-\!\!\!-\xi$

and here the letter 'ξ' is merely a place marker which marks the 'gap' or 'hole' into which the name of an object or of a truth-value may be inserted. The second element in (2) is

(4) $\varDelta$

which is just such a *name*. In the *Begriffsschrift* Frege stipulates that signs such as (4) must represent 'the conceptual content of a possible judgement' (*Bs*.2), though in the *Grundgesetze* this doctrine was modified so that the functional sign (3) could take *any* referential name in its argument-place. The third and final element in (2) is the small vertical stroke which occurs to the extreme left of the sign. This is the so-called 'judgement stroke' (*Urteilsstrich*) and when it is added to a functional sign that has been completed by an object name in its argument-place (i.e. a sign of the form: '$-\!\!\!-\!\!\!-\!\!\!-\varDelta$'), the resulting sign (2) *asserts* that (4) is a name of the True. Needless to say, at this point the nature of, and justification for these distinctions must remain obscure. But even at this point we can note that Frege has provided a

---

[8] I refer to Frege's booklet of 1879 as 'the *Begriffsschrift*' and to the perspicuous notation or ideography which it outlined as 'the concept-script'.

series of signs which enable us to represent an *object* ('*Δ*'); a *concept*
('———— *ξ*'); an object's falling under a concept, i.e. a *truth-value*
('———— *Δ*'); and an *assertion* ('|———— *Δ*'). And here we have the
basic concepts needed in a theory of judgement. Moreover, in laying
down the syntax and semantics for the concept-script, and in differ-
entiating the latter from the language of common discourse, Frege is
led to ask such questions as: What is a judgement? How does one
assert something? What is it for an object to fall under a concept?
When two people assert the same thing, what, if anything, do they
have in common? How is understanding related to assertion and
truth? Now, just such questions as these, and Frege's answers to
them, will be our concern in the present work.

CHAPTER I

FUNCTIONS AND REFERENCE

1. FUNCTIONS AND ORDINARY LANGUAGE

'IT is, even now, not beyond all doubt what the word "function" stands for . . .' wrote Frege, not without a certain melancholy, some eleven years after the publication of *Funktion und Begriff* and the *Grundgesetze der Arithmetik*. For it was in these works that Frege had outlined what he took to be a definitive solution to this problem. These works, however, fell dead-born from the press; and the article 'Was ist eine Funktion?', of which the quoted observation constitutes the opening words, was a renewed attempt on Frege's part to set out clearly and cogently what might well be regarded as one of his most important doctrines: the *Ungesättigtheit der Begriffe*, the unsaturatedness of concepts.

In the last analysis, however, the article was no more successful than its predecessors, and Frege eventually admits that although he is convinced of the truth of his doctrine of the unsaturatedness of concepts, still 'no definition is here possible. I must confine myself to hinting at what I have in mind by means of a metaphorical expression; and here I rely on my reader's agreeing to meet me half way.' (*Funk*.665.)

Now, as if this were not trouble enough, the only argument which Frege advances in this article for the conclusion that concepts are essentially 'unsaturated' or 'in need of completion' gives every appearance of being quite strikingly bad. Having so defined a function-*name* that it is essentially incomplete, by explaining that a function-name is what is *left over* after one or more occurrences of a singular term have been removed from a complex complete name, he then states:

The peculiarity of functional signs, which we here called 'unsaturatedness' has of course (*natürlich*) something corresponding to it in the functions themselves. They too may be called 'unsaturated'. (*Funk*.665.)

The aim of the present and immediately subsequent chapters is to offer an interpretation and, with some modification, a defence of the

Fregean doctrine of the unsaturatedness of functions. It will be shown that Frege's theory constitutes an important contribution to the solution of the puzzles concerning the phenomenon of sentential or propositional unity.

The first task is to introduce some terminology in which to explain Frege's account of functions, and the theory which underlies it.[1] Let us begin, then, with the intuitive notion of a *simple complete name*, i.e. an expression which either names or purports to name a determinate object and which contains no proper part which fulfils or purports to fulfil this function. Expressions like 'Socrates', '9', and 'Pegasus' fall into this category. A *complex complete name* is an expression which names or purports to name a determinate object, but which contains as a proper part a complete name, e.g. 'the wife of Socrates', '9²', and 'the stable of Pegasus'. Usually a complex complete name will name an object distinct from that named by any component complete name; 'the wife of Socrates', for example, names Xantippe. But this need not always be the case. 'Socrates' son's father', for example, refers to Socrates. The relation in which a complete name stands to the object which bears it Frege calls *Bedeutung*, a term which is variously translated as 'nominatum', 'denotation', 'reference' 'standing for', and 'meaning'. With the exception of the first and last of these terms, which I shall not use at all in this connection, I shall use all these terms interchangeably. Reference, denotation, and standing for will always stand in sharp contrast to the *sense* (*Sinn*) which an expression expresses.

At this point it is necessary to introduce two doctrines which Frege propounded concerning complex complete names. The first is this: the reference of a complex complete name is determined by the references of its component parts. We shall have cause to mention this principle for the determination of complex reference below, and can refer to it as *PR1* for short. It is impossible to understand *PR1* fully until the issue of the reference of incomplete expressions has been settled; still, one corollary of *PR1* can be noted immediately: if a complex complete name contains a component name which lacks a reference, then the complete name in which it occurs will also be

---

[1] The terminology is, on the whole, Fregean. I have, however, preferred the term 'predicate' to the more cumbersome and Germanic 'concept-word' (*Begriffswort*), and have borrowed the terminology of simple and complex complete names from M. Furth's Introduction to his translation of Frege's *Grundgesetze*.

without reference. If 'Pegasus' does not refer to anything, then neither does 'the stable of Pegasus'.

The second doctrinal assumption involved in Frege's account of the nature of functions is this: sentences are to be construed as a species of complex complete name. Sentences, if they possess a reference, refer to their truth-values. Thus, just as '9' is a simple complete name of the number 9, and '9²' is a complex complete name of the number 81, so '9²=81' is a complex complete name of the truth, and '9²=80' a name of falsehood. (Frege says that these sentential names are names of *the True* and *the False* respectively.)[2]

In conjunction with the corollary to *PR1*, noted above, this rather implausible theory results in the more intuitively acceptable claim that any sentence which contains a complete name that lacks a reference will be without a determinate truth-value:

The sentence 'Odysseus was set ashore at Ithaca while sound asleep' obviously has a sense. But since it is doubtful whether the name 'Odysseus', occurring therein, has a reference, it is also doubtful whether the whole sentence has one. (*SuB*.32.)

We can now turn to what is to be our central concern: *incomplete expressions* or *function-names* (*Funktionsnamen*). A function-name may be obtained by deleting or excising one or more complete component names from a complex complete name. The place or places formerly occupied by the excised names are marked either by pairs of empty brackets, or by use of the lower-case Greek letters 'ξ' and 'ζ'. Removal of the complete component name 'Socrates' from the complex complete name 'the wife of Socrates' leaves the incomplete expression 'the wife of ξ' (or 'the wife of ( )'). Removal of the complete name '9' from the complex name '9²' leaves the incomplete expression 'ξ²' (or '( )²'). And, because sentences have been construed as a species of complete referring expression, removal of the complete name 'Aristotle' from 'Aristotle was born in Stagira' leaves the incomplete expression 'ξ was born in Stagira', and so on.

Now Frege maintains that incomplete expressions generated in this way are also referring expressions. Although at this point it may seem an empty gesture, even granted that it is intelligible, I shall

---

[2] This is, it must be admitted, a most implausible doctrine. It will be examined critically—and dismissed—in the sequel (see Chapter I, §6 and Chapter II, §§5, 6 below). For the moment I simply present the theory without criticism or comment.

adopt the convention of designating that to which a given incomplete expression is supposed to refer by dropping the inverted commas and italicizing the resulting expression. And so, analogously to saying

'Aristotle' refers to (the man) Aristotle

I shall say

'ξ is a horse' refers to (the function) ξ *is a horse*.

This latter statement, then, is a superficial and provisional gloss on the Fregean thesis that functions are unsaturated. Functions, just like function-names, have, in Miss Anscombe's happy phrase, 'holes in them'.[3] To say this is not to offer a solution to anything, however, but is merely to state the problem with which we must deal.

Finally, in the matter of terminology, the object referred to by the complete name which is inserted into the gap in a function-name is called the *argument* of the function; and the reference of the completed function-name is called the *value* of the function for that argument. And so the function ξ^2 yields the value 4 for the argument 2, and the value 81 for the argument 9. First-level functions, it is beginning to emerge, perform the role of mapping objects (as arguments) on to objects (as values). It is also clear that those function-names which result from sentences map objects (as arguments) on to truth-values (as values). Such function-names would normally be called predicates and relational expressions. Frege calls that subclass of function-names which take truth-values as their values *Begriffs-wörter* or predicates; and such expressions are said to refer to unsaturated entities called *Begriffe* or concepts.

2. THE CONCEPT-SCRIPT

All that has thus far been said about functions and concepts applies to the language of common discourse and to the ordinary formulae of arithmetic. Throughout his life, but especially at the time of writing the *Grundgesetze*, Frege manifested a profound mistrust of ordinary language and the linguistic habits of mathematicians. He did not, of course, deny that for everyday purposes everyday language was entirely adequate. He was convinced, however, that for the expression of scientific truth, the vagueness, the ambiguity, and the contradictions which are present in ordinary language make it a most unsuitable medium. The first task in the construction of a rigorous science,

[3] G. E. M. Anscombe, *Introduction to Wittgenstein's Tractatus*, p. 109.

he believed, was the formulation of an adequate, perspicuous notation, a concept-script, from which all the infirmities of ordinary
language had been removed. As Frege wrote in the *Begriffsschrift*:

In my formalized language . . . only that part of judgements which affects
the *possible inferences* is taken into consideration. Whatever is needed for
a valid inference is fully expressed; what is not needed is, for the most part,
not indicated either; *no scope is left for conjecture*. (*Bs*.3.)

In particular, there are three desiderata which Frege tailored his
concept-script to embody: (i) determinateness of sense for all signs;
(ii) possession of reference by all signs (i.e. the possession of reference
by all complex signs built up according to the rules of syntax out of
simple signs which have reference); and (iii) perspicuity of logical
syntax. It is generally agreed that Frege's ideography met these ideals
as far as can reasonably be demanded. It was Frege's determined
pursuit of these goals which lead to his invention of quantificational
theory, of a truth-functional account of the logical connectives, of a
theory of logical types, and of the need for a rigorous distinction
between talking about a sign, what the sign means, and the object, if
any, to which it refers. History has, however, judged that Frege's
concept-script is not as perspicuous as the Peano–Russell notation,
and that it is cumbersome and expensive to print. Russell, whose
notation was to supplant Frege's, reacted in 1903 in a way which was
to prove virtually universal: 'His [Frege's] symbolism, though
unfortunately so cumbrous as to be very difficult to employ in
practice, is based upon an analysis of logical notions much more
profound than Peano's, and is philosophically very superior to its
more convenient rival.' (*PMs*.501.) Still, one cannot but have
sympathy with Frege's somewhat testy reaction to contemporary
criticism: 'After all,' he wrote, 'the convenience of the typesetter is
certainly not the summum bonum!'[4]

The element which, above all, gives Frege's concept-script its
distinctive and initially rather bewildering appearance is the system
of vertical and horizontal lines which initiate all well-formed
formulae within it. We must examine two of these lines if we are to
understand Frege's theory of functions. An example of a complex
proposition from the concept-script would be as follows:[5]

[4] 'Über die Begriffsschrift des Herrn Peano und meine eigene', p. 364. (Trans.
by V. H. Dudman, p. 3.)
[5] Fig. 1 is the concept-script representation of what today would be written as:
$(A \supset B) \supset (\Gamma \supset {\sim}\varLambda)$.

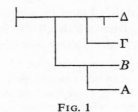

FIG. 1

Now *all* the horizontal lines in Fig. 1, and in the concept-script as a whole, perform the same role. A horizontal line is a function-name whose argument-place always occurs to its right, thus:

$$\text{——} \xi.$$

The function thus denoted, Frege tells us,[6] takes as its value a truth-value for any object as argument. It is, therefore, a concept. More precisely, Frege stipulates that

$$\text{——} \varDelta$$

shall be a name of the True if '$\varDelta$' is a name of the True; in all other cases it shall be a name of the False. And so 'we can say that

$$\varDelta = (\text{——} \varDelta)$$

is the truth-value of: $\varDelta$ is a truth value. Thus ——— $\phi(\xi)$ is a concept, and ——— $\phi(\xi, \zeta)$ a relation, whether or not $\phi(\xi)$ is a concept or $\phi(\xi, \zeta)$ a relation.' (*Gg*.§5.)

This is, indeed, rather obscure. But there is a tendency amongst commentators to obscure matters still more by divorcing the horizontal function-name from other predicates of a more usual sort, such as

ξ is now alive.

Dummett, for example, writes that the horizontal 'in effect turns any singular term into a sentence' (*FPL*.315). And Thiel writes that it 'makes possible the direct transition from objects, $\varDelta$, to truth-values, ——— $\varDelta$'.[7] This makes the horizontal stroke appear to function like a magic wand which, merely by appearing before a name can transform it into a sentence. For while 'Julius Caesar' is the name of a man,

——— Julius Caesar

is a name of the False!

[6] See *Gg*. §5 and *FuB*.21–3.
[7] C. Thiel, *Sense and Reference in Frege's Logic*, p. 53.

In fact, the matter is by no means as obscure or implausible as this kind of account would make out. For, in a certain sense, *all* predicates transform names into sentences. And just as 'Julius Caesar' is the name of a man, so

Julius Caesar is now alive

is a name of the False. In other words, the predicate '——— ξ' behaves in an exactly similar way to the predicate 'ξ is now alive'. There is, however, one difference between the horizontal stroke and an ordinary predicate like 'ξ is now alive' which can be brought out by remarking that in the former but not in the latter case there is *necessarily only one object which falls under the concept*. In other words, while any number of objects fall under the concept ξ *is now alive* (e.g. Richard Nixon, Gerald Ford, and many million others), there is necessarily but one object which falls under the concept ——— ξ, viz. the True. The horizontal stroke must, therefore, be read as an identity predicate, whose ordinary language equivalent, I suggest, would be:

ξ is identical to the True.

If this reading is accepted (and it will need only slight subsequent modification[8]), then the truth conditions of the function ——— ξ can be seen to follow immediately and intuitively: the value of the function will be the True if and only if the argument is the True. The value will be the False, moreover, not only when the argument is the False but also when the argument is not a truth-value at all! And so it is now clearly and unproblematically *false* that Julius Caesar is identical to the True, i.e. that

——— Julius Caesar.

It is now possible to understand the force of Frege's remark that '$\Delta = ($——— $\Delta)$ is the truth-value of: Δ is a truth-value'. The prefixing of the horizontal stroke to any name of a truth-value will in no way alter the reference of this name: any name of the True will remain a name of the True, and so, *mutatis mutandis*, for any name of the False. All other kinds of complete name, however, will be transformed into names of the False. And this means that it is impossible for a well-formed concept-script formula to lack a reference (a truth-value) as long as the complete names inserted in the gap after the

[8] See text corresponding to footnote 9 below.

horizontal stroke have a reference, *whatever* that reference might be. In this way Frege banishes from the concept-script not only all propositions which do not possess a determinate truth-value, but also all possibility of a non-sentential name masquerading as a 'possible content of judgement'. Critics who have objected that Frege's notation allowed the formulation of nonsense like '⎯⎯ 2' and '⎯⎯⎯ Julius Caesar' on the grounds that it is senseless to talk about 'asserting that 2' or to dispute over 'the truth of Julius Caesar' have failed to appreciate the ingenuity and the motivation for the horizontal stroke, which was introduced precisely to avoid the possibility of such syntactically malformed nonsense.

At this point two more concept-script function-names can be introduced:

(1) the small vertical stroke which hangs below a horizontal stroke, thus:

$$\overline{\top}\xi$$

is so defined that it is to have the value False if the argument is the True, and in all other cases it is to have the value True. It clearly corresponds to the ordinary language predicate

ξ is not identical to the True.

This small hanging vertical stroke is Frege's *negation sign*.

(2) a long vertical line which joins two horizontals is called the *conditional sign* (c):

The conditional sign is so introduced that 'the value of this function is to be the False if we take the True as the [ξ]-argument and at the same time take some other object as the [ζ]-argument; in all other cases it is to have the value the True.' (*FuB*.28.) In the 'exploded' diagram, above right, the lines *a* and *b* are the horizontals which attach directly to whatever names are inserted into the argument-places 'ξ' and 'ζ'. It is to these horizontals that the vertical conditional stroke *c* attaches. The horizontal stroke *d* then attaches to the whole thus formed. The whole complex sign illustrated above is, then, the equivalent concept-script representation of the ordinary incomplete expression 'If . . . then . . .'. (The place marked 'ξ' is the antecedent, and that marked 'ζ' the consequent.) But there is one important difference between an ordinary language conditional schema, and the Fregean conditional function-name: the latter, like all function-names, is to be defined for *all* objects as argument; the former schema is, of course, not. And so while

If the Eiffel Tower, then Julius Caesar

is just nonsense, the complex sign

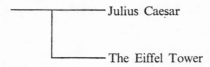

is actually true! This, as we have shown, is easily explained once the function-name '———— ξ' is read as 'ξ is identical to the True'.

3. THE JUDGEMENT STROKE

In order to complete our account of the nature of function-names in the concept-script, it is necessary to introduce another special Fregean symbol, but one that is not, and cannot be used to form, a function-name. This sign Frege calls the judgement stroke and it consists in a small vertical line which occurs to the left of the horizontal:

There are three things to note in connection with this sign: (i) it can only occur to the left of the dominant horizontal in a complex sign. It cannot, in other words, occur more than once in any complete sign, and cannot be prefixed by any sign whatever. (ii) It cannot occur in a function-name; and, because of the way in which function-names were introduced, this means that any sign in which it occurs cannot be a name. (iii) Its presence indicates that the signs which follow it are employed *assertively*. Signs of the form '├———— Δ' cannot be proper names, Frege maintains, and hence cannot be used to form function-names because they signify *assertions*; and clearly it is impossible to assert either a proper name or a function-name. The sign '├———— ξ', which would result from treating '├———— Δ' as a proper name capable of generating functional expressions, would have to signify (*per impossibile*) that 'ξ' was being asserted. But 'ξ' is merely a gap holder in an incomplete expression, and is not the sort of thing that can possibly be asserted. All this Frege summarizes in a troublesome footnote, to which we shall have cause to return on a number of occasions:

> The judgement stroke cannot be used to construct a functional expression; for it does not serve, in conjunction with other signs, to designate an object. '|——— $2+3=5$' does not designate anything; it asserts something. (*FuB*.22n.)

What, then is the difference between the two signs

(1) ——— $2+3 = 5$,

and

(2) |——— $2+3 = 5$?

It would appear, if we take literally Frege's contention that (1) is a name of an object (the True) while (2) is an assertion that something is the case (that $2+3 = 5$), that the difference between (1) and (2) is analogous to that between, say,

(3)   Dr. Smith

and

(4)   Smith is a doctor.

(1) and (3), we are tempted to say, are names; (2) and (4) are assertions. Now this comes, indeed, close to the truth. There is also, however, a sense in which (1) is not a name, and (4) is not an assertion. According to the analysis given above, (1) will be equivalent to '$2+3 = 5$ is identical to the True'; and this certainly does not look like a *name*, but rather a sentence. But then, if (1) is a name, but somehow at the same time a sentence, why should not the same thing also hold of (4)? In which case the intended contrast between names and assertions collapses. The way out of this difficulty is to amend the reading of the horizontal stroke so that the intended contrast becomes clear.[9]

Now, for Frege (1) is a name; we can be sure of that. It is the name

[9] This is the modification promised in the text corresponding to footnote 8 above.

of a truth-value which necessarily results when the function-name
'────── ξ' is completed by any sign that has reference, in this case:
'2+3 = 5'. The reference of the completed function-name is, however, precisely a truth-value, and this would incidate that its nature
is, *in some way, sentential*. But at the same time it is entirely lacking
in assertive force. Now there exists in ordinary language a type of
expression which conforms exactly to these requirements. The
nominalization of an indicative sentence is (usually[10]) without
assertive force, and yet is 'in some way sentential' in that a simple
grammatical transformation can render its sentential form explicit.
Consequently the function-name

$$────── \xi$$

ought to be interpreted, not as the identity sentence mentioned above,
but rather as the corresponding complex noun phrase:

ξ's being identical to the True.

In this form, to repeat, it is clear (i) that a nominal role is intended,
(ii) that assertive force is absent, and yet (iii) that a simple grammatical
operation will always yield a sentence (e.g. by the addition of the
phrase '. . . is a fact'). This account, then, will destroy the temptation
to say that if (1) is a name then (4) must be a name too. They are
obviously of quite different form.

The foregoing remarks were suggested by the following passage
from an article in which Frege compares his concept-script with that
of Peano's:

In the formula

$$(2 > 3) \supset (7^2 = 0)$$

a sense of strangeness is at first felt, due to the unusual employment of the
signs ' > ' and '='. For usually such a sign serves two distinct purposes: on
the one hand it is meant to designate a relation, while on the other hand it
is meant to assert the holding of this relation between certain objects.
Accordingly it looks as though something false $(2 > 3, 7^2 = 0)$ is being
asserted in that formula—which is not the case at all. That is to say, we must
deprive the relational sign of the assertive force with which it has been
unintentionally invested.[11]

[10] As P. T. Geach has noted, there are exceptions to this generalization. 'John's
being aware of the fact that p' does seem to contain the covert assertion that *p
is* a fact. Cf. P. T. Geach, 'Assertion', p. 453.
[11] 'Über die Begriffsschrift des Herrn Peano und meine eigene', p. 377.

Now the obvious way to divest a relational sign of its assertive force is to employ a noun phrase (R's obtaining) and not a sentential form (R obtains). It is important to note, however, that such grammatical transformations are not possible in the concept-script or in the formulae of logic or arithmetic. In arithmetic the expression

(5) $2+3 = 5$

must double not only for

(6)   2 plus 3's equalling 5

but also for

(7)   2 plus 3 *does* equal 5.

Frege, then, introduces the two expressions

(8)   ——— $2+3 = 5$

and

(9) |——— $2+3 = 5$

to correspond to (6) and (7) respectively. 'This is a manifestation', wrote Frege, 'of my desire to have every objective distinction reflected in my symbolism.'[12]

My intention at this point is not to embark upon a detailed examination of the concept *assertion*, nor of the uses to which Frege's judgement stroke can be put. These topics were introduced here only in order to show that a nominalized reading of the horizontal better suits Frege's intentions than one that is overtly sentential. In so far, therefore, as there are other uses to which the judgement stroke can be put, and other distinctions which the two sign types '——— $\varDelta$' and '|——— $\varDelta$' can be used to mark and which are not mentioned here, Frege's motivation must needs remain obscure. This matter will be taken up again in Chapter III below.

4. REFERENCE

The procedure which Frege typically employed to isolate those concepts necessary for an adequate semantics was what I shall call the

———
[12] Ibid.

procedure of noting invariance under substitution. The classical example of this method is to be found in the opening paragraphs of the essay 'Über Sinn und Bedeutung', where the reference of an expression is distinguished from its sense by noting that there are *two* things that may change (or remain the same) when different terms are substituted in an identity statement. One such variant is the truth-value of the sentence, and it appears that the truth-value of an identity statement will not vary as long as co-referential terms are substituted. But in the process of substituting co-referential terms, clearly something else *is* changed. This is especially clear in the case where the identity statement is of the form 'a = a', and one term with the same reference as 'a' is substituted to yield a statement of the form 'a = b'. Although 'a = a' and 'a = b' will have the same truth-value, they are 'obviously statements of differing cognitive value' (*SuB*.25). While the former is merely an instance of the principle of identity and can be known *a priori*, the latter may well contain 'substantial information'. If, however, terms are substituted which have the same cognitive value, then the cognitive value of the whole will be unchanged. This cognitive value is called by Frege the sense (*Sinn*) of an expression. The sense of a sentence Frege calls a Thought (*Gedanke*).[13]

Now the notion of the reference of an expression has thus far been treated as having a sufficiently clear intuitive content to enable us to proceed without scrutinizing this content too closely in its own right. And surely this assumption is justified when it is the reference of singular terms that is at issue. The reference of a singular term is that object which is picked out or named by the expression. But Frege so extended the notion of reference that for him it makes sense to ask of *any* expression of a given grammatical type, 'What is its reference?' Not only proper names, but predicates, sentences, and even logical connectives were also construed by Frege as referring expressions. Here one's pre-theoretical intuitions are of no avail; we need a semantical theory *in terms of which* we can understand such questions as: 'To what does the word "and" refer?' and 'What is the reference of the sentence "Julius Caesar is dead"?'

From the point of view of Fregean scholarship the matter has another problematic aspect. In the later works which Frege published

---

[13] These are only preliminary remarks. For a more detailed treatment of the notion of sense, see Chapter II.

during his lifetime (the three parts of the *Logische Untersuchungen*[14]) we find, surprisingly, no mention of the doctrines, once so central, that sentences refer to their truth-values and function-names refer to unsaturated entities called functions or concepts. This is enough to raise the suspicion that these doctrines are not ultimately as important as Frege made out in the middle period; for Frege is able, in the *Logische Untersuchungen*, to propound most of his important theories without any recourse or reference to them. The only passage in which Frege even hints that he continued to maintain this doctrine concerning reference in the works published after 1906 appears in 'Der Gedanke', where he writes, somewhat enigmatically:

> The meaning of the word 'true' seems altogether unique. May we not here be dealing with something which cannot, in the ordinary sense, be called a property at all? (*Ged.*61–2.)

However, he then immediately adds:

> In spite of this doubt I want first to express myself in accordance with ordinary usage, as if truth were a quality, until something more to the point can be found. (Ibid.)

Nothing 'more to the point' is to be found, however, in the remainder of the essay, nor in the subsequent parts of the *Logische Untersuchungen*, published or unpublished.

But perhaps Frege is being disingenuous. For the documents which compose the *Nachlass* reveal that as late as 1919 he had *not* abandoned the doctrine:

> On the other hand, not only a sentence part, but also a complete sentence whose sense is a Thought can have a reference. All sentences which express a true Thought have the same reference; and all sentences which express a false Thought have the same reference (the *True*, and the *False*).[15]

Now this makes it plausible to suppose that Frege did not change his mind on this central question, but merely refrained from mentioning the theory in the works which he published after 1906. To what can this reticence be attributed? Dummett has suggested that Frege's

---

[14] The *Logische Untersuchungen* comprise the three articles 'Der Gedanke. Eine logische Untersuchung' (1918), 'Die Verneinung. Eine logische Untersuchung' (1918), 'Logische Untersuchungen. Dritter Teil: Gedankengefüge' (1923), and also, perhaps, the posthumously published essay 'Logische Allgemeinheit', written in 1923 and first published, in *Nach.*, in 1969.

[15] 'Aufzeichnungen für Ludwig Darmstaedter', in *Nach.*276.

move here was a 'strategic one', and that he was 'leaving the notion of reference for later introduction' (*FPL*.660–1). Frege was well aware, Dummett argues, that his theories of sentential and functional reference were very far from plausible, and consequently were likely to alienate those who might otherwise take an interest in his work. Now such speculation about Frege's psychological motivation is, I suggest, profitless. Such speculation tells us nothing about Frege's philosophical theories; and it remains, moreover, ultimately unsubstantiated guesswork. There is, however, another way in which Frege's reticence in this matter can be interpreted; one which throws some light on his philosophical motivation.

In the *Begriffsschrift* and in the works which comprise the middle-period Frege is almost exclusively concerned with the pure, formal sciences (logic, arithmetic) and with the development of a concept-script that would adequately embody their truths.[16] The works published after 1906 are of quite a different character. No longer is the emphasis upon 'pure thought' and the concept-script, but rather upon scientific thought and language *in general*. And this includes both pure and applied science. Now, by a scientific language—or better: a scientific use of language—Frege means simply one which is 'directed towards the truth, and *only* the truth' (*Ged*.63). This, therefore, includes not only the tautologies of logic and the analytic truths of arithmetic (if such they be) but, indeed, all sentences that are not fictitious, poetical, fanciful, or meant dishonestly. Frege mentions explicitly in this context: mathematics, physics, chemistry, and *history* (loc. cit.). Now if we take literally Frege's claim that

It is just as important to neglect distinctions that do not touch the heart of the matter as to make distinctions which concern what is essential. *But what is essential depends on one's purpose* . . . (*Ged*.64.)

then I think that it is possible to construe the absence of the theory of the *Bedeutung* of sentences and function-names as motivated by methodological considerations, determined by the increase in the scope of the investigation. The doctrine that a sentence denotes its truth-value assumed a central role in the attempt to axiomatize arithmetic, where, as Dummett has remarked, it 'permitted a great economy in Frege's classification of the denizens of his ontological universe: concepts . . . appeared as merely a special case of unary

---

[16] Frege's creative life divides naturally into three periods: the early period: until 1890; the middle period: 1890–1906; the late period: 1906–1923.

functions, and relations as a special case of binary ones; a concept is just a function whose value, for any argument, is a truth-value. This effected a certain streamlining in the formal system of *Grundgesetze* as compared with that of *Begriffsschrift.*' (*FPL*.644.) But when Frege turned to consider the language of general science, this theory was no longer needed to account for the phenomena under investigation. And for the same reason a special sign '|————' to mark the possession of assertive force is no longer required. For in ordinary, non-formal language, as Frege says, 'the real assertive force lies . . . in the form of an indicative sentence' (*Ged*.63).

It is plausible, then, to maintain that there was no doctrinal change on Frege's part, but merely a change in tactic. This was not, however, dictated by external considerations (e.g. a desire not to confuse or repel his readers) but resulted from the change in the character of the material upon which he was working.

All this, regrettably, tells us nothing as to the *truth* of the doctrine that sentences denote their truth-values. And we are left in the position of being committed to a doctrine which is obscure, highly implausible and, moreover, possibly unnecessary. The following considerations will, I hope, show that this doctrine is not an inescapable consequence of accepting a Fregean account of sense, reference, and judgement, etc. In other words, the theory that sentences and functional expressions are a type of *name* can be shown to be, in Wittgenstein's metaphor, a wheel which turns freely and is without connection with other parts of the mechanism. This conclusion is, indeed, suggested by the fact that Frege can say so much in his later works without any recourse to this doctrine. But to remain satisfied with this suggestion would be to leave open the very real possibility that Frege's cupboard contains a skeleton which might ultimately make the whole house uninhabitable.

Let us begin, then, with an examination of the Fregean doctrine that functional expressions, and predicates, *refer to* or *name* an unsaturated entity called a function, or concept.

For the sake of brevity I shall restrict my discussion to those function-names which have only one argument-place, and whose values are always truth-values. In other words, I shall talk only about *predicates* and *concepts*; though what I say is easily extended to cover, on the one side, relations, and on the other side, functions which are non-sentential. A predicate will always be a form of words of some sort, as will a name and a sentence. Concepts, relations, functions, extensions, Thoughts, and truth-values will never be words of any sort. We must now try to ascertain *what* these latter are, and *how* they are related to various forms of words.

Frege's doctrine concerning the relations which obtain between a predicate, its sense, its reference, and its extension is certainly the most obscure and puzzling area in Fregean semantics. The visible tip of this iceberg of obscurity is the seemingly paradoxical assertion that

the three words 'the concept *horse*' designate an object, but on that very account they do not designate a concept (*BuG.*195)

and hence that

the concept *horse* is not a concept (*BuG.*196).

At least part of the thought which receives such paradoxical expression is this: if one defines a proper name (*Eigenname*) as 'a sign for an object' (*BuG.*198n.), and one defines an object as 'whatever is not a function' (*Gg.*7), then it will follow, of course, that there can be no such thing as a proper name of a concept. The motive which prompts this set of definitions is that objects are complete in themselves, saturated or self-subsistent, while concepts are, by contrast, incomplete, unsaturated, and unable to stand by themselves. What does this mean? It means, in part, the indisputable truth that an object can never be predicated of an object. It also means that a list of names cannot assert a Thought, i.e. anything that could possess a truth-value. And it also means that a concept cannot fall under a concept of the same level. We must examine these claims in detail. We can begin by taking the predicate

(1)   ( ) is drunk[17]

as an example. Suppose that now a second predicate is introduced,

---

[17] (a) I here employ the alternative convention for marking the argument-place in a function-name or predicate, viz. an empty pair of brackets. There is, of course, no significant difference between 'ξ is drunk' and '( ) is drunk'.

(b) Strictly speaking, '( ) is drunk' is not a fully-fledged Fregean predicate; for the truth-conditions of the sentences which result from its completion by a proper name are indeterminate because (i) there is not time indication; (ii) the concept of drunkenness is vague; (iii) it is not normally defined for such objects as, say, numbers or pieces of furniture. The nature of, and rationale for these requirements are examined below pp. 42ff.

such that it applies to all and only those objects to which (1) applies. So any completion of this predicate, viz.

$$(2) \qquad\qquad (\ ) \text{ is } \phi$$

by a referring expression will result in a sentence of the same truth-value as the sentence which results from the completion of (1) by that same expression. (1) and (2) are clearly co-extensive. Perhaps, it might be thought, (1) and (2) both denote the same concept. But it is just this suggestion which Frege denies is even a meaningful hypothesis. For it to be meaningful, he argues, it must be possible to formulate an identity statement of the form

$$(3) \qquad\qquad (\ ) = (\ )$$

and in which the gaps are occupied by terms denoting concepts. But this cannot be done; for

$$(4) \qquad\qquad (\ ) \text{ is drunk} = (\ ) \text{ is } \phi$$

is nonsense. And

$$(5) \qquad\qquad \text{'( ) is drunk'} = \text{'( ) is } \phi \text{'}$$

is simply false. Indeed, expressions of the same form as (5) will be false for any two typographically differing expressions as terms in the identity statement. 'Identity, properly speaking, does not apply to concepts,' concludes Frege. But he goes on to add: 'coincidence in extension is a necessary and sufficient condition for the occurrence between concepts of the relation *corresponding to* identity between objects'.[18] But if this is the case, why not take the simplifying step of

[18] In more technical terminology, ( ) = ( ) is a first-level relation which can take only *objects* as arguments. The 'analogous' relation for *concepts* Frege writes thus:

(i) $\qquad \vdash\!\!\!-\!\!\!-\!\!\!-\!\!\!\overset{\mathfrak{a}}{\smile}\!\!\!-\!\!\!-\ \phi(\mathfrak{a}) = \psi(\mathfrak{a})$

or

(ii) $\qquad \vdash\!\!\!-\!\!\!-\!\!\!-\!\!\!-\!\dot{a}\phi(a) = \dot{\epsilon}\psi(\epsilon).$

Expression (i) would today be written as

(iii) $\qquad (x)(\phi x \equiv \psi x).$

Expression (ii) asserts the identity of the *Wertverläufe* of the functions $\phi(\ )$ and $\psi(\ )$; and the closest Russellian rendering is

(iv) $\qquad \hat{x}(\phi x) = \hat{x}(\psi x).$

See, further, below, pp. 147–154. The quotation is from Frege's Review of Husserl's *Philosophie der Arithmetik*, p. 327.

identifying a predicate's reference with its extension? There would then be no need to resort to the strange notion of an unnameable but objectively real unsaturated entity, or 'concept', which a predicate denotes.

In the first place, it is clear that the extension of a concept-word or predicate is not its sense, for when co-extensional predicates are interchanged in a sentential context the Thought expressed by the sentence may change. Thus, '( ) is a chimera' and '( ) is a unicorn' share the same extension, though they do not yield sentences expressing the same Thought when completed in the same way. (Not that there is the slightest intuitive reason to think that they would or should.)

An argument of the same form is not, however, available to show that the reference and extension of a predicate are different. For, at least in Frege's extensional system it *is* the case that co-extensional concepts can be interchanged *salva veritate*. How, then, does Frege think that he can prize apart the notions of reference and extension?

In the realm of reference, what a name denotes and what a predicate denotes must always and absolutely be distinguished: 'I do not want to say it is false to assert of an object what is . . . asserted of a concept; I want to say it is impossible, senseless to do so' (*BuG*.200.) This senselessness is manifest in the syntactical malformedness of the (putative) sentences which result from an attempt to predicate a concept of a concept of the same level; i.e. to treat a concept-word as a proper name. We noticed this malformity in connection with expressions like (4) above. The reason for this malformity is simply that English sentences do not have holes in them, and Fregean predicates do. Two alternatives suggest themselves at this point: either the hole can be rendered harmless, by enclosing the expression in inverted commas; or the holes can be filled in. The first alternative does not enable us to treat a concept as an object, for we end up referring to an expression, and not to the concept we intended (as in (5) above). The second alternative, filling in the hole, looks at first sight more promising. Is not the predicate (1) just *one* way of referring to that concept which is *also* denoted by the expressions 'drunkenness' and 'the concept *drunk*'? For Frege, as we have already seen, the possibility of substitution *salva veritate* is the criterion for ascribing sameness of reference to two or more expressions. But neither of these two alternative expressions can be substituted for (1) as it occurs in, say,

(6)   Julius Caesar is drunk.

For the expressions which result:

(7)   Julius Caesar drunkenness

and

(8)   Julius Caesar the concept *drunk*

are not sentences. No such complete names can be substituted for an incomplete predicate, because the result is a *list* not a sentence.

This, then, is the background to the 'paradox of the concept *horse*', as it has come to be known. Frege is forced to say that 'the concept *horse* is not a concept' because the expression 'the concept *horse*' is not a predicate, is not an incomplete expression denoting a function, but a complete expression which thus denotes an object. And an object cannot enter into immediate logical combination with another object. It is the problem of propositional unity which forces upon Frege what he calls 'an awkwardness of language' whereby, for any concept $\phi(\ )$, it is never the case that the concept ϕ is a concept.

5. SOME OBJECTIONS

There are a number of objections to the foregoing reconstruction of some Fregean theses concerning concepts which may well have occurred to the reader, and which it will be profitable to deal with at this point. In the first place, as Dummett has remarked, it might well be thought that Frege has confused talk about signs with talk about what those signs refer to. Once Frege's paradox about the concept *horse* is framed in the formal and not the material mode it ceases to be problematic:

There is no more paradox in the fact that the *expression* 'the grammatical predicate "is red"' is not a grammatical predicate, than there is in the fact that the phrase 'the city of Berlin' is not a city. In the material mode of speech Frege was forced into such at least superficially contradictory expressions as 'the concept *horse* is not a concept' . . . but when we are talking about expressions then we have no motive for denying the obvious fact that 'is a horse' is a predicate, nor for affirming the obvious falsehood that the phrase 'the predicate "is a horse"' is a predicate.[19]

In other words (W. Marshall's words): 'Frege has taken a linguistic difference to be a rift in nature.'[20]

[19] M. A. E. Dummett, 'Frege on Functions; a Reply', p. 97.
[20] W. Marshall. 'Frege's Theory of Functions and Objects', p. 390.

Another response is that the whole question of 'unsaturatedness' would not arise if the convention of marking the 'gaps' in predicates were not adopted, or, again, if nominalized transformations were allowed to be co-referential with the paradigm predicates from which they result. In other words, it can appear tendentious to claim that the predicate which occurs in the sentence 'Julius Caesar is drunk' is *this*:

(9)   ( ) is drunk.

For one thing, the expression (9) does not even occur in the quoted sentence. And, finally, even granted that such expressions as (9) are in order, this hardly entails that such formulations are the only ones possible. There are occasions (so the objection runs) when we want to assert something *of a concept*, and here the concept must needs appear as subject and in a nominalized form, as e.g. in the sentence 'Drunkenness is undesirable'.

Objections such as these manifest a misunderstanding of Frege's theory of functions: of his distinction between marks (*Merkmalen*) and qualities (*Eigenschaften*); between concepts of first and higher levels; between an object's falling under a concept (and the analogous *subter* relation), the subordination (*Unterordnung*) of one concept and another (and the analogous *sub* relation), and the falling of one concept within another concept of higher level. The following account of these Fregean doctrines is meant to be only as complete as is necessary in order to deal with the forementioned objections. Much remains to be said about the finer points of Frege's theory that is, however, not germane to the present task.

There are three distinct and dominant, and two subsidiary and derivative relations which together constitute the formal nucleus of Frege's theory of functions and concepts:

I.   *falling under*   (holds between an object and a concept)

II. *subordination*   (holds between two concepts of the same level)

III. *falling within*   (holds between concepts of levels n and $n+1$)

and

(i) ξ *subter* ζ (where ξ is an object and ζ is a class)

(ii) ξ *sub* ζ (where both ξ and ζ are classes)

Relation I is that relation in which an object stands to a concept when the concept maps it on to the True. Or, less technically, it is the relation of elementary true predication. Julius Caesar falls under the concept ( ) *is now dead*, for example, because it is true that Julius Caesar is now dead. Relation (i) is analogous to I, only it holds between an object and a class, not between an object and a concept. Thus Julius Caesar is a member of the class of things now dead. '*x subter α*' would today be written as '$x \in α$'.

'Subordination' is the relation which obtains between two concepts of the same level when all the objects which fall under the first also fall under the second: the first (somewhat surprisingly) is then said to be subordinate to the second. In general, if it is the case that $(x)(\phi x \supset \psi x)$, then ϕ is subordinate to ψ. A special case of the relation of subordination is the relation which obtains between a concept and its mark(s). In this case subordination is the converse of the relation which Kant and traditional logicians called 'inclusion'— a relation which is captured by analytic judgements. Under the traditional theory, the concept *bachelor*, for example, contains or includes the concept *unmarried*. The concept *bachelor* is in this case subordinate to the concept *unmarried*; the latter is a mark of the former. In general, if it is analytic that $(x)(\phi x \supset \psi x)$ then ψ is a mark of ϕ (*BuG*.201–2).

Relation (ii) is the analogue of II, holding between classes rather than concepts. If two classes, α and β, are such that α *sub* β, then any member of α is a member of β: $(x)(x \in α \supset x \in β)$. If α is the extension of the concept ϕ and β is the extension of the concept ψ, and if α *sub* β, then it will be the case that $(x)(\phi x \supset \psi x)$. But this latter may well be a merely contingent truth. This is not always understood. In the introduction to his translation of Frege's articles concerning the foundations of geometry, for example, E. W. Kluge writes that 'the relation between properties and concepts is such that whatever is a property of an object is a characteristic [or mark] of the concept under which the object falls' (p. xvii). Well, Julius Caesar falls under the concept *man*; Julius Caesar has the property of having been murdered on the ides of March; but the concept *man* does not have the mark: *murdered on the ides of March*. Otherwise we would all know what end necessarily awaited us! What Frege actually says is 'whatever is a mark of a concept is a property of an object which falls under that concept'—*not* vice versa. (Letter to Liebmann, in *Brief*. 150. Cf. *BuG*.201.)

Relation III, that of *falling within*, is one of the most important tools for the implementation of Frege's logistic programme; for it plays a quintessential role in his account of *number*, of *existence*, and of *generality*. The relation is that between a concept, ϕ, and another concept Ω, such that ϕ is of level-n, Ω is of level-$(n+1)$, and 'Ω' signifies a property possessed by ϕ. As an object may fall under a concept, so a concept may fall within a higher level concept.

'The fundamental part of my result', wrote Frege in the introduction to the *Grundgesetze*, 'is expressed . . . by saying that assignment of a number involves an assertion about a concept; upon this my present work is based.' *Cardinality*, in other words, is a second-level concept within which first-level concepts are said to fall. To assert that there are three coins in the fountain is to assert of the concept

(10)   ( ) is a coin in the fountain

that it possesses this property (falls within this second-level concept): *has three instances*. Having three instances is clearly a property of concepts, not of objects; for it is nonsense to talk about objects having instances. Likewise it is nonsense to predicate number of objects—despite the great grammatical similarity between the sentences involving genuine first-level predication (relation I) and those involving ascription of a property to a concept (relation III). Compare, for instance, the superficially similar sentences:

(11)   The coins in the fountain are three

and

(12)   The coins in the fountain are dirty.

In (12) the concept ( ) *is dirty* is asserted to have falling under it each object that also falls under the concept ( ) *is a coin in the fountain*: if an object is a coin in the fountain then it is dirty. But the logical form of (11) must be different. 'If an object is a coin in the fountain then it is three' makes no sense at all. But if number cannot be asserted of objects, it cannot be asserted of classes, groups, or aggregates of objects either. The class of objects which are coins in the fountain is not three, any more than are its members. Indeed, for Frege, a class *is* an object. It is not to the class of ϕ things that number is ascribed, but to the concept ( ) *is a member of the class of ϕ things*. It is this concept which may have the property of having three instances.

Under Frege's analysis *existence* is also a second-level concept within which first-level concepts fall: 'in this respect existence is analogous to number. Affirmation of existence is nothing but denial of the number nought' (*Gl*.65). To assert that there exist flying saucers, for instance, is to assert of the concept ( ) *is a flying saucer* that the number of objects falling under it $\neq 0$.

There can be little doubt, however, that Frege's greatest single contribution to logic was the provision of a precise notation for, and consistent theory of, the logic of quantification. Indeed it was possession of such that enabled Frege to give the foregoing account of cardinality and existence. As we have already seen, Frege substituted for the traditional subject/predicate analysis of judgement one which proceeded in terms of functions and their arguments. But the immense explanatory power of this new form of analysis is by no means fully revealed by a consideration of elementary sentences (such as 'Caesar is drunk') for which the subject/predicate and the function/argument analyses largely coincide. Pre-Fregean analysis typically divided such a sentence into a subject ('Caesar'), a predicate ('drunk'), and the copula which unites them. I have argued that even when applied to such elementary sentences the analysis in terms of an incomplete function-name and its complete argument is greatly superior to its traditional rival. This superiority is, however, fully revealed only when we come to consider judgements involving relation III. Take, for example, the sentence

(13)   Some men are myopic.

This was traditionally construed as comprising the predicate 'myopic', the copula, and the subject 'some men'. One peculiarity of this analysis is brought out by considering how such a sentence is negated: the negation of (13) is not 'Some men are not myopic', but 'No men are myopic'. And here we seem to be negating the subject and not the predicate. But if we subscribe to the plausible doctrine that (in Geach's words) 'when a proposition is negated, the negation may be taken as going with the predicate in a way in which it cannot be taken to go with the subject',[21] then the traditional theory collapses; for 'some men' cannot be both the predicate and the subject of one and the same sentence. Frege solves this conundrum by denying flatly that (13) is of subject/predicate form, and by providing an alternative account according to which both (13) and

(14)   All men are myopic

[21] P. T. Geach, *Reference and Generality*, p. 32.

are examples of a first-level concept's being said to fall within a second-level concept.

The sentential function-name '$\phi(\xi)$' is obtained from the (closed) sentence '$\phi(a)$' by the removal of the singular term 'a' and the insertion into the remaining gap the letter 'ξ', which merely holds open the argument-place in this function. What happens if instead we remove the sign 'ϕ' from our original sentence? If we adopt the convention of marking the place from which we have excised a first-level function-name with the dummy letter '$\varXi$', then the result is the second-level function-name '$\varXi(a)$' (which might be rendered roughly as: $\varXi(\ )$ is a concept under which object a falls). Frege introduces the universal quantifier as a second-level concept which we symbolize as:

(15)   ———$\underset{\smile}{a}$——— $\varXi$ (a)

Here again '$\varXi(\ )$' merely marks the argument-place of this function— a gap which can take only first-level functions of one argument. (15) can be read as: $\varXi(\ )$ is a concept under which all objects fall. The indentation in the horizontal stroke is the sign for universal generality; the gothic 'a' above it, in association with the occurrence of that same letter in the argument-place of the first-level function to the right of the horizontal stroke, delimits the scope of the generality. So the function (15) yields the value *false* for the argument: ξ *is edible*. When 'ξ is edible' is inserted into the place held by '$\varXi(\ )$' there results the expression

(16) |———$\underset{\smile}{a}$——— a is edible

where the bound variable 'a' occupies the gap held by 'ξ'. This is the concept-script representation of the judgement that everything is edible, which asserts of the first-level concept ξ *is edible*, that it falls within the second-level concept: $\varXi$ *is a concept under which all objects fall*.

|——$\underset{\smile}{\overset{a}{|}}$——| a is edible

is the concept-script representation of the existentially quantified judgement that there exists something that is edible (i.e. that not everything is inedible).

The problem of multiple generality is solved by the invention of an iterable sign for generality combined with a precise means of indicating the scope of any such sign. And this latter is the procedure of binding variables.

Brief though they are, these considerations enable us to see that certain of the foregoing objections to Frege's theory of functions are misguided. Kerry's objection that a concept can also be an object, because a concept can occur as the subject of an act of predication, involves a confusion of logical levels or types. If the nominalized predicate expression occurring as the subject of such a sentence as

(17)   Drunkenness is undesirable

is construed as referring to a concept, then the sentence must be analysed as possessing the form of relation III. In which case (17) may be expanded, albeit somewhat picturesquely, to read: 'ξ is drunk is a concept which ought to have no instances'. Here the unsaturatedness of the subject concept is made manifest, the temptation to view 'drunkenness' as the name of an object is destroyed, and the predicate is clearly seen to represent a second-level concept which takes first-level concepts as its arguments. If, on the other hand, 'drunkenness' is taken to refer to an abstract object then 'ξ is undesirable' must be taken to denote a first-level concept. In other words sentence (17) may be analysed either as an example of relation I or of relation III. Kerry's objection is only plausible when these two relations are conflated. And, parenthetically, we might mention here the obvious relevance of these considerations for Ramsey's well-known objection to the doctrine of the irreducibility of particulars and universals.[22] For there is no reason why we should not analyse the statement made by the sentence 'Socrates is wise' as either an example of relation I or of relation III. In the former case the object Socrates is said to fall under the first-level concept ξ is wise; in the latter case this first-level concept is said to fall within the second-level concept: what Socrates is Ξ. And here a simple monogrammatical union will yield: what Socrates is is wise, which is just another way of saying that Socrates is wise. But this by no means tends to show, as Ramsey thought, that there is no final difference between objects and concepts. For, to repeat, relation III obtains between concepts, not between an object and a concept.

It was suggested above that Frege's struggles with the concept concept could simply be avoided by formulating the theory in the

22 F. P. Ramsey, 'Universals' in The Foundations of Mathematics, pp. 112–34.

formal and not the material mode. If this were done, it was suggested, it would be nonsense to say that 'the concept *horse* is not a concept'; but what this remark is trying to say could be formulated thus: 'the predicate "is a horse"' is not a predicate. And *this* is certainly true. Now this objection is one which will have considerable force for those, following Tarski and Carnap, who find the distinction between object language and metalanguage(s) clear, illuminating, and inescapable. Frege, however, like Wittgenstein, made no *radical* distinction between talking about extra-linguistic entities and talking about languages. They did not, of course, confuse talking about the weather with talking about 'the weather'; but the difference here is merely a difference in subject-matter and not a radical difference in the type of language being employed. Both philosophers, moreover, denied that ultimately any philosophical problem could be solved by an appeal to a metalanguage, even one which possessed a wider vocabulary than, or different semantical rules from, the object language under discussion. As far as concerns the case before us—the nature of predication—whatever problems arise over the object language predicate '( ) is a horse' will arise over the metalanguage predicate '( ) is a predicate'. (Does it denote a concept? Is it unsaturated? Is it defined for all objects? Does it express a determinate sense? And so on.) As van Heijenoort has shown,[23] Frege did not follow Boole and De Morgan in restricting his concept-script to an arbitrary universe of discourse which would comprehend 'only what we agree to consider at a certain time, in a certain context. For Frege it cannot be a question of changing universes. One could not even say that he restricts himself to *one* universe . . . Frege's universe consists of all that there is, and it is fixed.' But then expressions are just as much objects in the world, objects possessing properties and standing in relations with other objects, as are tables and chairs. To say that '( ) is drunk' is a predicate is to assert of the *object* '( ) is drunk' (which happens to be an expression) that it falls under the *concept*:

( ) *is a predicate.*

If our objective is to understand the relations which obtain between objects and concepts, then an appeal to a hierarchy of languages will be of no avail.

Finally, it was objected that to ask for the sense or the reference of the expression '( ) is drunk' is a futile exercise; for *this* expression is

[23] J. van Heijenoort, 'Logic as Calculus and Logic as Language', pp. 324–30.

not an expression of English, and certainly does not occur in the sentence 'Julius Caesar is drunk'. Now one could argue here that people normally have little need to refer to predicates in isolation, and so natural languages tend to lack any clear conventional way of doing this. We are free, therefore, to introduce our own conventions here; and the convention adopted has the built-in heuristic device that it indicates the place where a singular term or a bound variable may be substituted so as to yield a sentence. But this is too glib to have any explanatory value. More light is shed on the nature of predicate expressions by the following suggestion by P. T. Geach, which, though perhaps based more on a reading of the *Tractatus* than on the writings of Frege, is none the less entirely Fregean in character. Geach argues that a predicate is, strictly speaking, not an expression, not a typographically identifiable object which can be displayed by itself within quotation marks. It is rather 'a common property of expressions':

... when I say that 'Booth shot Lincoln' and 'Booth shot Booth' contain the common predicate 'Booth shot ——,' I do not mean that the expression last quoted occurs in both sentences; plainly it does not, for neither sentence contains a dash! What I mean is that the two sentences have the common property of being related in the same way to the expression 'Booth shot ——'; viz., each of them is obtained by substituting a uniquely referring name for the dash in this expression; and this common property *is* the common predicate.[24]

In Fregean categorial grammar there are two kinds of complete or 'saturated' expression: sentences and proper names. Function-names (of which sentential function-names, or predicates, are a subclass) are, on the other hand, 'unsaturated'. Geach's suggestion gives us, at last, a means of dispensing with these metaphors—at least as far as expressions are concerned. A proper name and a sentence simply *are* expressions; whereas a predicate is not: a predicate is a property of expressions. In so far as an expression is an object whose identity conditions are merely typographical (phonetic etc.), its Fregean status as 'self-subsistent' is unproblematic. A property of an expression, however, is not self-subsistent but is, precisely, a property *of* some object.

There is much more to be said about predicates and their 'unsaturatedness' but this must be postponed for the moment. The topic will be taken up again in Chapter II.

[24] P. T. Geach, 'Quine on Classes and Properties', p. 410n.

We must now attempt to answer the question: Why ought predicates to be construed as a species of referring expression? It might well seem that this question can hardly arise for us: if a predicate is not an expression it cannot, *a fortiori*, be a referring expression. This is not quite right, however, for although a predicate is not, strictly speaking, a typographically identifiable entity, we will nevertheless want to speak of a predicate's expressing a sense. And if this is to be possible we ought not to be so cavalier as to dismiss outright the possibility of its possessing a reference. Moreover, the kinds of consideration which Frege adduced in support of his claim that predicates refer apply equally to the above account of the nature of predicates, which is, indeed, merely a partial interpretation of what he calls their 'unsaturatedness'.

Frege's procedure for assigning references to sentences is, as we have seen, to look for that which remains invariant when co-reverential terms are interchanged. This—or at least, one such—invariant turns out to be the truth-value of the sentence. The justification of this procedure is the basic principle for the determination of complex reference (*PR1*) that the reference of a complex complete name is determined by the references of its component parts.

Now this principle works well when the component parts whose reference is in question are singular terms. So it is that Frege can claim with great plausibility that the reason that the sentence 'Odysseus was set ashore at Ithaca while sound asleep' is without a reference (a truth-value) is that at least one of its parts ('Odysseus') is without reference (*SuB*.32). Of course the sentence is by no means meaningless or useless; it expresses an intelligible sense. Frege then asks why it is that the sense is not enough for us; and he answers: 'Because, and to the extent that, we are concerned with . . . truth-value. It is the striving for truth that drives us always from the sense to the reference' (*SuB*.33). Now if 'reference' is to mean for predicates even approximately what it means for singular terms, then there must be some property which a predicate may possess, and the absence of which will deprive any sentence in which it occurs of a determinate truth-value. But it is difficult to conceive what this property might be, over and above the possession by the predicate of an unambiguous *sense*. To the question: What would it be like for a predicate to possess a sense but lack a reference? there seems intuitively to be no answer. For certainly it cannot be replied that a predicate's reference is the conceptual extension: empty concepts can with perfect propriety be used in the most rigorous of scientific languages. Frege himself insisted on this very point. In the posthumously published fragment 'Ausführungen über Sinn und Bedeutung', where, having argued that proper names which do not refer to anything *must* be banished from a scientific language, he writes:

Concept words without a reference must also be rejected though this does not exile those that are self-contradictory—for a concept can legitimately be quite empty—but, rather, *those whose borders are vague*. (*ASB*. in *Nach*.133.)

Concepts whose borders are vague, Frege maintains, are without reference. This, then, is the work expected of the notion *reference* as it applies to predicates.

It is beginning to emerge that Frege has not one, but two notions of reference. These notions hang together so well in the case of singular terms that they are hard to distinguish in this context. In the case of predicates, however, they are not only distinguishable, they are difficult to reconcile. One notion is this: the reference of an expression is that extra-linguistic entity with which the expression has been correlated or which it picks out. The other notion of reference is that it is a property which an expression must possess if that expression is to be *truth-valuable* (to coin a phrase). By truth-valuable, I mean such that it either possesses a truth-value, or is capable of being used (and not just mentioned) in a sentence which possesses a truth-value. We have seen that vacuous singular terms are not truth-valuable. Indeed being truth-valuable in the case of proper names just *is* possessing reference in the other sense, i.e. 'being directed to an object'. Precisely what is implausible in Frege's theory of predicate reference is the idea that there is *something to which* predicates refer, and *not* that there should be some property which they may possess and in virtue of which they are truth-valuable. Frege never clearly distinguished these two notions either for proper names (which is understandable) or for predicates (which is puzzling). He wrote as though being truth-valuable was a clear indication that an expression was correlated with some extra-linguistic entity. We shall have to see if these two strands in Frege's thought are related in the way Frege obviously believed them to be, and if not, whether either is worth salvaging.

This is how Frege specifies the property which a predicate, or indeed any functional sign, must possess if it is to be truth-valuable:

> A name of a first-level function of one argument has reference . . . if the proper name that results from the filling of the argument-place of this function-name always has reference, just as long as the name substituted has reference. (*Gg*.i.46.)

Or, again,

> It must be certain, for every object, whether or not it falls under the concept; and any concept-word that fails to meet this condition of referentiality is referenceless. (*ASB*. in *Nach*.133.)

This doctrine is very far from intuitively obvious. How is this notion of a concept's having sharp borders related to the more usual notion of reference? It is, I believe, possible to show that these two notions are linked by an important analogy which Frege can take credit for discovering. It is to be doubted, however, that this analogy is strong enough to justify extension of the term *reference* so as to cover predicates and other incomplete expressions.

As we saw earlier, Frege's notion of a concept is introduced and explained via the operation of removing from an assertive sentence one or more occurrences of a singular term. In this way the notion of a predicate's being true of an object is explicated in terms of the truth of the sentence which results from the completion of the predicate by any name of that object. Sentences refer (if they refer) to their truth-values; and Frege never tires of insisting that there are two and only two of these; *tertium non datur*. Sentences which refer neither to the True nor to the False do not, therefore, refer at all. But now, if concepts are allowed which do not meet the condition of sharpness, this whole doctrine is threatened. For if a given concept, $F(\ )$, is undefined for an object, a, then the sentence '$F(a)$' will not have determinate truth conditions and will not succeed in referring. This state of affairs directly threatens the principle of reference *PR1*, whereby the reference of a complex expression is a function of the references of its component expressions. For that the function-name '$F(\ )$' has both a sense and a reference is proved by there being just one true *or* false sentence in which an object is said to satisfy it. If, say, '$F(b)$' is true (or false), and the proper name 'a' has a reference, then '$F(a)$' must also have a reference. And so predicates must be everywhere defined if they are anywhere defined. The analogy, mentioned above, is that a predicate which is everywhere defined (if it is anywhere defined) is truth-valuable in just the way in which a proper name is truth-valuable if it is 'directed towards an object'. That predicates must have sharp boundaries is an especially important demand for a concept-script which allows of unrestricted universal quantification; if the predicate 'F( )' is undefined for just one object, a, then the universal statement '$(x)F(x)$' will also be without a determinate truth-value.

Is the subsumption of predicates under the category of referring expressions, then, just a peculiar demand of the concept-script, with little or no relevance to everyday thought and language? One thing is clear: the vast majority, perhaps even all, of the predicates employed in the language of common discourse lack the absolutely sharp limits which Frege demands.

Throughout Frege's works there are general and more or less dogmatic assertions of the need for all concept-words to be defined for all objects as arguments. There is, however, so far as I know, only one place at which he subjects this doctrine to the scrutiny which it obviously deserves. The examination occurs in the *Grundgesetze*, vol. II, (§§ 62–5), and it is fair to say that the arguments advanced by Frege in favour of his conjecture are almost entirely negligible.

Frege approaches the issue via the suggestion that the range of function-names might be restricted, so that functions would not need to be defined for all objects. The function

$$(18) \qquad\qquad ( )+( ) = 1$$

for example, need not possess a value for the arguments: *the sun* and *the moon*. One could surely restrict substitution in (18) to the natural numbers. To this suggestion Frege has a number of objections. In the first place he argues that before substitution could be thus restricted, we should first have to be in possession of a watertight definition of the concept *number*: 'We may indeed specify that only numbers can stand in our relation . . . But with that would have to go a complete definition of the word "number", and that is just what is most lacking.' Basically Frege's objection is not that such a definition is theoretically impossible, but merely that it would be rather difficult to formulate:

If people would actually try to lay down laws that stopped the formation of such concept names as this [i.e. 'The sun + the moon = 1'] which, though linquistically possible, are inadmissible, they would soon find the task exceedingly difficult, and probably impracticable. (*Gg*. II, §64; *G&B*.168.)

Frege's argument seems to be an argument from laziness: we ought to define all concepts for all objects because this is less of a task than formulating the restrictions that would otherwise be necessary. But this is false. It is Frege who owes us an explanation of what the sense and the reference of such an inappropriately completed function-name is. Of course it is possible to stipulate *ad hoc* what Quine calls a 'don't care' value for inappropriate substitutions. It is not generally realized, however, that this stipulation must accord with and be based upon the *prior* and clear distinction between what is and what is not an appropriate substitution. In the example we have been using, before it can be stipulated that for non-numerical substitutions the function (18) is to have the value the False, or Quine, or the null set, or whatever, we must be in possession of a clear distinction between what is and what is not a number. And if such a distinction is *already* available then there is no reason why, *pace* Frege, it cannot be employed to rule out non-numerical substitutions altogether. Frege's weak argument to the effect that formulating restrictions on substitution instances is an 'exceedingly difficult task' is one which seems to have gained wide acceptance. Geach, for example, writes as follows:

'What is $(\!(+2$?' [where '$(\!($' refers to the Moon]; the answer is a matter of arbitrary stipulation; 'the only point of a rule to this effect is that there should *be* a rule'. . . . For Frege, every complex designation must have a reference, if it is to be well formed; so we can deny a reference to designations like '$(\!(+2$' only if we are going to have formation rules that exclude them from our language. The framing of such rules in a water-tight way is a *much heavier business* than stipulations which would supply a reference for this sort of designation—say, the stipulation that when the signs preceding and following the *plus* sign do not both stand for numbers [*sic*] the whole expression has the same reference as the sign preceding the *plus* sign, so that '$(\!(+2$' would designate the Moon, and '$2+(\!($', the number 2.[25]

Now such *ad hoc* stipulations are not so easy to produce as Geach seems to think. In the first place, under the token stipulation given in the last sentence of this passage, it would no longer be true that, e.g.

$$(x)\,(y)\,(x+y = y+x).$$

And if this proposition is to be true, then we must have a rider to the effect that *substitutions must be numerical*; but the argument was designed to show that such restrictions are impracticable. This,

[25] G. E. M. Anscombe and P. T. Geach, *Three Philosophers*, p. 148 (my italics).

however, is a small point. Much more important is Geach's remark (immediately preceding '[*sic*]') that stipulation is only necessary when non-numerical signs are substituted in an arithmetical function-name. Now, no stipulation is possible when the names substituted in '( )+( )' are '2' and '3' respectively. For the value of '2+3' *is* 5. If I 'stipulate' that it shall be 3 then I am simply making a mistake, and introducing an element of anarchy into arithmetic. If anarchy is to be avoided, there must be a foolproof way of distinguishing those cases in which *ad hoc* stipulation is necessary, from those in which it is not allowed. But if such a criterion is already available, there can be no objection to employing it to *outlaw* expressions of the former type, instead of forcing an interpretation on them. To outlaw such expressions as meaningless is much more in keeping with the way we normally use language; for an expression like '(+2 = Geach' ought to turn out to be senseless on any account! If it is senseless then it cannot have a reference (a truth-value), and merely stipulating a reference does not thereby provide a complex expression with a sense.

In brief, then, there is no substance to this objection to restricting possible arguments of functions. Apart from anything else, this objection relies on the validity of a distinction which it is the very purpose of the argument to deny.

Frege has one more argument to show that any restriction on the domain of substitution is impossible. This argument is independent of the one examined above, and runs as follows:

Let us suppose for once that the concept *number* has been sharply defined; let it be laid down that italic letters are to indicate only numbers . . . By a well known law of logic, the proposition
if *a* is a number and *b* is a number, then a+b = b+a
can be transformed into the proposition
if *a*+*b* ≠ *b*+*a* and *a* is a number, then *b* is not a number
and here it is impossible to maintain the restriction to the domain of numbers. (*Gg*.II, §65; *G&B*.169.)

The conclusion which Frege draws is that 'the force of the situation works irresistibly towards the breaking down of such restrictions'. If the situation has any force, then it is considerably stronger than Frege realizes; for it works towards the destruction of *all* categorial boundaries whatsoever, including those which Frege would wish to keep intact (e.g. the distinction between objects and concepts). Consider, for example, the exactly parallel argument in which it is assumed that italic letters range over *all* objects unrestrictedly. It will then be true that

if *a* is an object and *b* is an object then $a+b = b+a$;

but by a well-known law of logic, this can be contraposed to yield

if $a+b \neq b+a$ and *a* is an object, then *b* is not an object.

This ought to show that the categorial difference between objects and functions is untenable. But there is something radically wrong with a statement like '*b* is not an object': it breaks the *syntactical* rules under which we are working. It cannot 'turn out' that *b* is not an object; 'b' is a *sign for* an object. It is evident that something is here amiss; if we accept Frege's mode of argument, it will commit us to a type-free and absolutely homogeneous syntax and ontology. I do not know if this idea is intelligible, but it was certainly far from Frege's mind. Just what has gone wrong here Wittgenstein was one of the first to diagnose, in the *Tractatus*. He argued that paradox and nonsense results when *formal* concepts (*object, function, number, concept*) are treated as common or garden *material* concepts. If the concept *object* is employed to mark a syntactical type, then the putative predicate '( ) is an object' will not function like a material concept, say, '( ) is an elephant'; for the former will be true of everything that can meaningfully be substituted in it. Any attempt to apply the predicate '( ) is an object' to what is not an object will result not in a false sentence, but in a syntactically malformed expression. Wittgenstein argued that in a consistent and perspicuous language, that something was an object, a function, a number, etc. was *shown* in the symbolism employed, and could not be *said*. Frege adopted this view as far as concerns functions: that something is a function is shown by the incompleteness of the sign used to refer to it; but '( ) is a function' is an impossible sign combination. Frege, however, never extended this doctrine to include '( ) is an object', nor did he acknowledge the possibility that there might be other formal concepts. There is, I have suggested, no good reason why he should not do either of these things.

The arguments which we have examined so far in support of the claim that predicates refer have been, so to speak, indirect arguments, designed to show that for a predicate to have reference is for it to be defined for every object whatever, and that, at least in a 'scientific language', truth-valuable predicates must possess this property. There is only one occasion on which Frege argues at any length directly that there must be some extra-linguistic entity with which a predicate must be correlated. This occurs in the posthumously published piece (written in 1906) 'Einleitung in die Logik', and is interesting in that it shows how very literally Frege took his talk of the 'realm of reference' and the 'realm of sense'. For Frege these were no mere *façons de parler*, but ontological categories encompassing objective entities:

It is immaterial to the mere thought content [expressed by a sentence] whether a proper name has a reference; but this is of paramount importance, at all events, in so far as one's concern is scientific. . . . Now it is indeed unlikely that a proper name should be so different from the remaining part of a singular sentence that the possession of a reference would be of importance for it alone. On the contrary, we must take it that if the whole thought belongs to the sphere of truth, then something in the realm of reference corresponds to that remaining part of the sentence whose sense is the unsaturated part of the thought. In addition to which, in this remaining part of the sentence there may also occur proper names whose reference is important. . . . The sense of each of these proper names can be contrasted as a complete part to the remaining unsaturated part of the thought. . . . When we say 'Jupiter is larger than Mars', about what are we speaking? About the heavenly bodies themselves, about the references of the proper names 'Jupiter' and 'Mars'. We are saying that they stand to each other in a certain relation; and we do this with the words 'is larger than'. This relation obtains between the references of the proper names and so must itself belong to the realm of reference. (*Nach*.209.)

As plausibility arguments these are rather unconvincing. There are three of them: (a) that because predicates and proper names function in what is, prima facie, so similar a manner, in the absence of any evidence to the contrary they must both be presumed to be referential. (b) Because an object can constitute a *part* of a concept, and (c) because concepts *hold of* objects, both objects and concepts must belong to the same ontological realm: the realm of reference.

Argument (a) need not detain us: there is no plausibility in the claim that predicates and proper names function in semantically similar ways. On the contrary, a name is *correlated* conventionally with an object; a predicate, on the other hand, may be *true of* various objects, just one object, or no objects at all. Moreover, as Dummett has remarked, while the role of a proper name is to pick out an object, 'The role of a predicate is not to pick out a concept' (*FPL*.244). In the next chapter we will present an alternative account of predication—one which does not invoke the notion of predicate reference. Argument (b) is invalidated by the inapplicability of 'part/whole' terminology to the relation between a function and its argument (see below, p. 51). The third argument depends upon the dubious attribution of references to sentences. But even if, for the moment, we allow this, the argument still does not go through. For it is simply a *non sequitur* to say that if a function maps an object (reference) on to a truth-value (reference) then the function too must belong to the realm of reference.

7. SUMMARY

The gist of these observations is that there seem to be no good reasons for demanding, with Frege, that function-names and predicates have a determinate value for all objects as arguments. But, as this is a necessary and sufficient condition for their being said to refer, these considerations also tell against the doctrine that function-names are a species of referring expression.

The tenor of these remarks has not, however, been entirely negative; for the crucial importance of the notion of *sense* is beginning to emerge. Quine, who believes that attempts to restrict quantification are misconceived, being based on accidents of language rather than on any purely logical considerations, would represent the Fregean statement that, for all objects whatsoever,

$$a+b = b+a$$

as

$(x)\,(y)$ (If x is a natural number, and y is a natural number, then $x+y = y+x$.)[26]

And Quine would say that the quantifiers here range over all objects, the necessary restriction being brought off internally, so to speak, by the antecedent of the conditional. And in the case in which x is Socrates, say, and y is the Moon, Quine would say we have a 'don't care' case, in which the antecedent is simply *false* and so constitutes no exception to the generalization. But this is a little slick. Quine owes us an account of how a senseless sentence can possess a truth-value. And if the expression 'If Socrates is a natural number and the Moon is a natural number, then Socrates plus the Moon is equal to

[26] e.g. W. v. O. Quine, *Elementary Logic*, §§32f.

the Moon plus Socrates' is not senseless, then Quine owes us an account of what its sense is. For, in Frege's words, a sign without a sense is 'just an empty series of sounds'; and the act of assigning a truth-value to an expression does not thereby give it a sense.

Frege is not consistent on this issue; but in what, it could be argued, are his more profound moments, he tends to emphasize that possession of a clear *sense* is the *sine qua non* of an expression's being used in a language of any sort:

A proper name must at least have a sense . . . otherwise it would merely be a series of empty sounds and wrongly called a name. A proper name stands for an object through the mediation of its sense and through this alone. A concept-word must also have a sense . . . and this applies, indeed, to *every* sign or complex of signs . . . (*ASB.* in *Nach.*135.)

Now this line of thought runs counter to that which claims that we can stipulate a *reference* for a nonsensical expression, and thereby introduce the expression unexceptionably into a language. But before we can fully appreciate the relative merits of these two approaches, we must examine the notion of *sense*.

CHAPTER II

FUNCTIONS AND SENSE

1. INTRODUCTION

W E introduced in the preceding chapter a principle for the determination of complex reference (*PR1*) which ran as follows: the reference of a complex expression is determined by the references of its component expressions, both complete and incomplete. Indeed, at times Frege uses the stronger language of wholes and parts, so that the reference of a complex expression is said to be *composed* of the references of the component parts. This led him (e.g. *SuB*.35) to maintain that a truth-value is a composite object made up of a concept and an object—a doctrine which it is easy neither to understand nor to accept. Frege eventually realized, however, that this formulation of *PR1* is quite unacceptable. For if the reference of the complex expression 'the capital of Sweden', say, is composed of the references of 'the capital of ( )' and 'Sweden', it would follow that Sweden is a part of Stockholm! (Cf. *Nach*.275.) The more acceptable formulation of *PR1* can be represented diagrammatically as in Fig. 2.

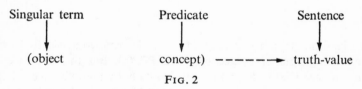

FIG. 2

PR1 is the principle upon which Frege primarily relies when he is examining scientific language and the concept-script. Elsewhere in his writings, however, he seems to invoke a quite different principle which we can call *PR2*. It is this: (a) the reference of any expression is determined by its sense, (b) the sense of a complex expression is determined by the senses of its component parts. *PR2* can be represented as in Fig. 3.

That Frege did not clearly distinguish *PR1* and *PR2*, even though he would invoke one rather than the other according to whether he was

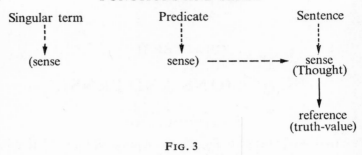

FIG. 3

writing about natural language or the concept-script, is shown by Fig. 4 which is based upon one contained in a letter from Frege to Husserl (May 1891). It is an incomplete amalgamation of Figs. 2 and 3 above:

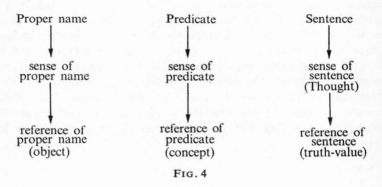

FIG. 4

In Fig. 4 the reference of the sentence is determined vertically by the sense of the sentence, according to *PR2*(a). But the reference of the sentence is also determined horizontally by the references of the component expressions, according to *PR1*. Clearly the reference of complex expressions (both sentential and sub-sentential) is over-determined. In the previous chapter we advanced reasons for rejecting *PR1*, either as unilluminating (when it demands that predicates denote unsaturated entities) or as false, at least for natural languages (when it demands that all predicates be defined for all objects). We must now examine *PR2* and ascertain whether or not it fares better than its predecessor.

It can be noted immediately that *PR2* is, intuitively, not only clearer than *PR1*, it is more plausible as well. That the truth-value of a sentence, or the reference of a complex expression such as a definite description, is determined by the sense of that sentence or expression, and that this, in its turn, is determined by the senses of the words which go to make it up, these are theses which seem scarcely disputable. They have, however, been disputed. The next section is an attempt to outline some of the problems which face any prospective theory of sense.

2. SOME PROBLEMS

Frege begins the essay 'Über Sinn und Bedeutung', in which the distinction between an expression's sense and its reference was first expounded, with the observation that '$a = a$' and '$a = b$' are obviously statements of differing cognitive value (*Erkenntniswert*)'. The opening paragraphs of this essay constitute, in effect, a distinction between the *cognitive-value* and the *truth-value* of a sentence. Thus, if 'a' and 'b' are two different names for one and the same object, then both '$a = a$' and '$a = b$' will be true; and they will be true for the same reason: the two terms flanking the identity sign stand for the same thing. The first identity statement is, however, trivially analytic, while the second 'may contain very valuable extensions of our knowledge' (*SuB*.25). It seems that the notion of sense, as it is introduced by Frege, is to be an epistemological notion. The sense of a declarative sentence will be, roughly, that which we understand when we understand the sentence. This is the interpretation which Dummett has recently given. 'What can a model of sense be', he asks, 'but a model of what it is to grasp a sense?' (*FPL*.293.) 'The notion of sense was required in the first place in order to explain how our sentences come to have the cognitive value which they have for us.' (Ibid. 240.)

Early in the article under discussion, however, Frege introduces a slightly different notion of sense: 'I should like to call the sense of a sign [that] wherein the mode of presentation (*Art des Gegebenseins*) is contained' (*SuB*.26). What is 'presented' is, of course, the reference of the expression. Now, regardless of how justifiable an explanation of sense along such lines may ultimately be, this notion cannot be used to *introduce* the concept of sense in general, i.e. for expressions of any type; for it has not yet been established what is to count as the reference of expressions other than proper names, if anything at all. Because the notions of predicate- and sentence-reference are quite without intuitive, pre-theoretical content, such notions cannot be used to introduce a theory which will then, in turn, explain them.

Nor is the language of cognitive value free of difficulties. In the first place it only seems appropriate to talk about the cognitive value of a sentence; for only a sentence can be understood, can contain information, can express knowledge, and so on. This is a point which Wittgenstein has expressed with rhetorical force as follows: 'Doesn't understanding only start with a proposition, with a *whole* proposition? Can you understand half a proposition?' (*PG*.39.) And yet Frege clearly intends that the notion of sense should apply univocally to proper names and predicates as well as to sentences. (The possession by predicate expressions of either sense or reference is nowhere mentioned in *SuB*. Frege was obviously reserving treatment of this topic for a second article, 'Ausführungen über Sinn und Bedeutung', which, however, he never published.[1])

Neither the account in terms of cognitive value, nor that in terms of the mode of presentation of a reference will suffice unamended to introduce and explain the general notion of *the sense of an expression*; for sub-sentential expressions do not possess cognitive value, and expressions other than proper names do not clearly possess reference.

There is another, more fundamental, difficulty confronting any attempt to formulate a coherent theory of sense, however: it is strangely difficult to say *what* the sense of an expression is. 'On hearing the assertion "This sentence makes sense" you cannot really ask "What sense?"' wrote Wittgenstein, 'Just as on hearing the assertion "This combination of words is a sentence" you cannot ask "What sentence?"' (*PG*.51.) And in an analogous way, the question 'What is the sense of the word "Aristotle"?' seems to defy explicit and precise answer. Some have thought this state of affairs evidence for the fact that there are no such things as senses. Russell wrote, in 'On Denoting':

The difficulty in speaking about the meaning [sense] of a denoting complex may be stated thus: 'The moment we put the complex in a proposition, the proposition is about the denotation . . .'

And here I must quote Searle's delightfully graphic account of how this is supposed to happen:

Imagine a game where marbles are dropped into bowls through pipes. This

[1] Cf. the editors' comments in *Nach*.128. The article was written at approximately the same time as *SuB*.

act is called referring. Pipes (senses) lead to bowls (references). It is a rule of the game that anything can be referred to. The difficulty is though that we cannot live up to this rule because we cannot refer to a pipe. Every time a marble drops into a pipe it goes through to the corresponding bowl.[2]

Now, as in fact Searle argues against Russell, this is not quite right. For we *can* refer to senses, and we do this in the way in which Frege indicated, by employing an expression of the form: the sense of the expression ' . . . '. It was just confusion on Russell's part which led him to deny this. But this does not clear up the difficulty, not mentioned by Searle, that we cannot say *what* the sense of an expression is. The closest we may approach to this is to say that the sense of a given expression E_1 *is the same as the sense of another expression*, E_2. There seems to be an interesting analogy here with certain difficulties concerning Fregean concepts: concept-words refer, but we cannot stipulate *what* it is they refer to. I shall return to this point shortly.

In addition to saying that E_1 has the same sense as E_2, we can also hint at or indicate what the sense of an expression is. 'Aristotle', we might say to someone who did not understand our use of the word, 'was a Stagirite philosopher taught by Plato.' And in so saying we would give our hearer *some idea* of what the sense of the word 'Aristotle' is. But it would be a grave mistake to construe such elucidations as precise stipulations of sense. For one thing, if 'Aristotle' is to have the same sense as one or more identifying definite descriptions of Aristotle, then such obviously contingent statements as 'Aristotle was taught by Plato' or 'Aristotle was born in Stagira' will turn out to be classically analytic. Russell and Bradley subscribed to versions of this peculiar theory; Frege did not. And yet there are those who would foist it upon Frege,[3] claiming that for him, as for Russell, a proper name is somehow 'equivalent to' or 'an abbreviation for' a definite description. This ascription seems to be based mainly on a footnote to 'Über Sinn und Bedeutung', where Frege writes:

In the case of an actual proper name such as 'Aristotle' opinions as to the sense may differ. It might, for instance, be taken to be the following: the pupil of Plato and teacher of Alexander the Great. Anyone who does this will attach another sense to the sentence 'Aristotle was born in Stagira'

[2] J. Searle, 'Russell's Objections to Frege's Theory of Sense and Reference', in *Klemke*, 341.

[3] Notably, e.g., P. T. Geach in *Three Philosophers*, p. 137 and S. Kripke in 'Naming and Necessity', p. 255.

than will a man who takes as the sense of the name: the teacher of Alexander the Great who was born in Stagira. (*SuB*.27n.)

Now it must be admitted that in this passage, confused and confusing though it is, Frege does seem to be giving the sense of a proper name by saying that it is a certain man: the pupil of Plato and teacher of Alexander the Great. This is nonsense, of course; though doubtless it was the origin of Russell's pseudo-problem about one's necessarily referring to the reference of an expression when what one had intended was the sense. But if Frege is not guilty of identifying the sense of the name 'Aristotle' with the man Aristotle, then what exactly is he saying? In other words, how are we to interpret the Fregean schema:

(1)   the sense of 'N' is: the ϕ?

Commentators have advanced two interpretations of this curious procedure. According to the first, Frege is subscribing to the theory that a proper name is a disguised definite description, and that schema (1) is most accurately read as:

(2)   the sense of 'N' is the same as the sense of 'the ϕ'.

But if the sense of an expression is the 'mode of presentation' of its reference, then it is impossible for a proper name to have the same sense as a definite description, precisely because the two types of expression present their reference in quite different ways: a name is not true of its bearer, not is a description arbitrarily correlated with an object.[4]

According to a different reading, (1) can be taken quite literally and involves no imprecision of expression on Frege's part; for it can be read as exactly equivalent to

(3)   'N' means the ϕ.

And here the verb 'to mean' introduces a phrase which has what Frege calls indirect reference. As we shall see in more detail later, an expression in an indirect context refers to what is normally its sense. And so, it is maintained, schema (1) does not identify the sense of a proper name with its reference, but, because the definite description occurs in an oblique context, with its sense. In fact, however, this reading is merely a variant of the first and would *identify* the sense of

---

[4] Frege himself insists on this point, *Ged*.66.

a name with that of some descriptive phrase—a doctrine which is not consonant with Frege's general account of sense and which has, moreover, unacceptable consequences in that obviously contingent statements turn out to be analytic.

Schema (1) ought, I think, to be interpreted literally; at least in that what is being specified is the *reference* of a proper name. And Frege, it must be admitted, gives every impression of believing that therewith the sense has been specified. Elsewhere, however, he is quite adamant that there is no backward road from reference to sense. What a completion of schema (1) achieves, then, is not the specification or identification of the sense of a proper name, but merely its *elucidation*. The distinction between a definition and an elucidation is Frege's (cf. 'On The Foundations of Geometry' (1906), p. 301) and is justified by the observation that if any definition is to be possible then there must be some primitive terms which are not defined; otherwise an infinite regress results. 'Since definitions are not possible for primitive elements, something else must enter in. I call it elucidation' (loc. cit.), which is an informal indication of the meaning of an expression. A specification of the reference of a proper name may constitute an elucidation of its sense; but for reasons given it cannot be a precise specification of that sense. As I shall argue below, it is not in fact possible to give *any* precise specification of the sense of a proper name—though this is no reason to deny that such expressions have a sense.

3. SENSE IN GENERAL

As a start towards the construction of a Fregean theory of sense, we can, somewhat negatively, begin by saying what sense isn't; that is, by distinguishing the sense of an expression from other ingredients in what might, with intentional vagueness, be called its 'meaning'. The categorization of semantically relevant factors in any language of reasonable complexity capable of expressing truths is effected by Frege in terms of the following five key concepts: *sense, reference, indication, colouration*, and *force*.

(i) The first thesis concerning senses is that they are objective. And this alone is sufficient to distinguish the notion of sense from what Frege calls 'colouration' (*Färbung, Beleuchtung*). Frege distinguishes two types of colouration; one consists in the subjective images, memories, and associations which a given expression may on a particular occasion cause to come before someone's mind:

> The ... sense of a sign is to be distinguished from the associated idea ... The same sense is not always connected, even in the same man, with the same idea. The idea is subjective: one man's idea is not that of another ... This constitutes the essential difference between the idea and the sign's sense. (*SuB*.29.)

To take an extreme example, the name 'Venice' may remind me of my last year's holiday. Only one who thought the sense of a sign is something mental and subjective would be tempted to claim that such imagistic associations were a part of an expression's meaning.

A second phenomenon which Frege includes within the notion of an expression's colouration is what today would be called its connotation. Although this concept is rather difficult to define exactly (Dummett has called it 'a rag-bag of a concept'), it is easily recognized on an intuitive level. It would generally be admitted that from the following pairs of terms either might be used in place of the other without appreciable change in meaning: 'dead' or 'deceased', 'old' or 'aged', 'bastard progeny' or 'illegitimate offspring', 'perspiring' or 'sweating'. What little difference in meaning there may be between the members of these pairs, it is not enough to alter the statement which one might make in employing one rather than the other. The differences are rather in nuance, suggestiveness, or sound. Frege is wrong to class this as a *subjective* phenomenon: the connotations of some terms are as objective and public as their senses. In fact, however, Frege does not need to call them subjective, because he has a more adequate and sharper criterion for distinguishing sense from colouration/connotation: the sense of an expression is that part of its meaning which is not its force, but which is what we earlier called 'truth-valuable'. In other words, all differences between two expressions which are too slight, too subjective, too vague to affect the truth-value of any sentence in which they occur are to be excluded from the sense of the expressions, and lumped under the term 'colouration'.

(ii) The notion of force (*Kraft*) applies only to sentences and sentential phenomena, and about this notion I shall have a great deal more to say in Chapter III. The remarks in the present section are intended merely as preliminary and provisional means of distinguishing between the sense and the force of an expression. Roughly speaking, then, it is in terms of the force with which it is used or uttered that we would distinguish between a sentence's being a question, an assertion, a promise, a command, the expression of a wish, or an example of a grammatical point. One and the same spoken sentence, say, 'I promise to make you pay the money', might possess any of these forces; tone of voice and context of utterance would normally indicate which force was intended. Sense, on the other hand, is a notion which attaches to sentences *per se*, and the sense of the sentence 'I promise to make you pay the money' will remain constant throughout such changes in force. This is because the force of a sentence is something which is only present when the sentence is used, uttered, or written on a particular occasion. To use a well-worn but still serviceable distinction: the sense of an expression is the business of semantics, its force the business of pragmatics.

(iii) The term *andeuten*, usually translated as 'indicate', applies to the way in which the variables of logic and arithmetic function. Variables are introduced in order to achieve generality, and in the equation 'a+b = b+a' the letters 'a' and 'b' stand indeterminately for any natural numbers. Frege introduced the technical term *andeuten* in order to combat the prevalent belief that variables refer to (*bedeuten*) a strange entity called a variable number. He was combatting the view that the two signs '2' and 'n²' function in the same way by denoting numbers, only that while '2' denoted a determinate number, 'n²' denoted an indeterminate number.[5] 'We cannot say that 'n' denotes (*bedeutet*) one indefinite number; but we can say that it indicates (*andeutet*) numbers indefinitely.' (*Funk*.659.) Frege points out that the indefiniteness attaches adverbially to the verb 'to indicate' and not adjectivally to the number(s) indicated. Signs which, like variables, only indicate but do not refer have, according to Frege, neither reference nor sense, outside a sentential context: 'We some-times use the expression "the number *n*", e.g. "If the number *n* is even, then cos $n\pi = 1$". Here only the whole has a sense.' (*Funk*.659.) 'Now what does 'x^2+3x' denote? Strictly speaking, nothing at all; for the letter "*x*" only indicates numbers and does not refer to them.' (*Funk*.663.) Clearly Frege construed variables as syncategoremata, incomplete symbols which are only meaningful when at work within a

[5] Russell remarks in 'On Denoting' that '"a man" denotes not many men but an ambiguous man'. Frege would no more countenance 'ambiguous men' than he would 'variable numbers'!

sentence; and in a sentence they only indicate and do not refer to their values.

(iv) These notions of colouration, force, and indication, as well as the notion of sense, can all be roughly classed as aspects of, or distinctions within, the notion of an expression's *meaning*. We come now to the notion of reference, and as Dummett has observed with considerable insight: 'Reference, as Frege understood it, is not an ingredient in meaning at all: someone who does not know the reference of an expression does not thereby show that he does not understand, or only partially understands, the expression.' (*FPL*.84.) Dummett then adds that, for Frege, reference 'is a notion required in a *theory of meaning*—in the general account of how language functions—just as the notion of truth is so required: but the reference of a term is no more part of what is ordinarily understood as its meaning than the truth-value of a sentence is.' (Ibid.) This contention is surely incontestable in the case of sentences and their truth-values: I can fully and perfectly understand the sentence 'The Empire State Building has 150 storeys', even though I am in total ignorance of its truth or falsity. But Dummett's contention does not so obviously apply to proper names.

4. PROPER NAMES

Can we say that I fully understand the name 'Julius Caesar' even if I do not know to whom or to what it refers? Here we must tread carefully; for although I believe the matter is quite simple, the history of recent philosophy is not without examples of those who have gone adrift over just this point, the most spectacular being Russell. Now, Russell notwithstanding, the verb 'to know' as it is used in the phrsae 'to know the reference of an expression' cannot be taken to mean to be *acquainted with*. For then the ridiculous conclusion would be that, being unacquainted with Julius Caesar, I could not understand such a sentence as 'Julius Caesar is now dead'. And, again Russell notwithstanding, the person Julius Caesar is no part to the meaning of the expression 'Julius Caesar', nor of any expression in which this occurs. For as Wittgenstein has shown, if he were then it would be the case that part of the meaning of the sentence 'Julius Caesar is dead' used to be bald, crossed the Rubicon, and is buried in Rome. But *meanings* do not cross rivers or lose their hair. Frege makes just this point in a recently published letter to Jourdain:

When we find the same word, say 'Etna', in two sentences we realize that there is also something common to the two Thoughts [thus expressed], something which corresponds to this word.... Now this part of the Thought which corresponds to the name 'Etna' cannot be the *reference* of this name. For if it were, of course, every lump of solidified lava that is part of Etna would also be part of the Thought that Etna is higher than Vesuvius. But it seems absurd to me that lumps of lava, and indeed other such things of which I have no knowledge, should be parts of a Thought. (*Brief*.127.)

The object referred to by a proper name is no part of the meaning or sense of that name.

On the other hand, however, it must be admitted that there is a strong temptation to claim that in order to understand the proper name 'Julius Caesar'—or, better, in order to understand sentences in which that name is used—one must know who Julius Caesar is. This temptation has its origins in the intuition that if 'Julius Caesar' occupies the subject position in a sentence, that sentence will be about Julius Caesar. But if one does not know who Julius Caesar is, but uses such a sentence, then, literally, one will not know what one is talking about. And so, the argument goes, the answer to the question: 'Can one be said to understand the sentence "Julius Caesar is dead" if one does not know who Julius Caesar is?' ought to be 'No'. And the result of this negative answer is the attempt to enrich the notion of the sense of a proper name, so that the sense specifies who or what the reference is, and anyone who *understands* the sense thereby *knows* who or what is referred to. This, as we saw above, was the approach adopted at one point by Frege: someone who knows the sense of the name 'Aristotle' thereby knows that Aristotle was the pupil of Plato and the teacher of Alexander the Great, or some such uniquely identifying description.

We have already seen why this cannot be right: if we say that the sense of the name 'Aristotle' is: the pupil of Plato, then we are identifying the sense with the reference of the name, *or* we are identifying the sense of the name with the sense of the definite description. And neither of these moves is admissible. Moreover, I can well understand sentences in which the name 'Aristotle' occurs without knowing that just *this* definite description applies uniquely to him. But, if the requirements of the theory are weakened so that *any* uniquely individuating description will here suffice, then the requirements no longer correspond to the intuitions that prompted them;

for knowing one obscure fact which happens to be true of Aristotle and nobody else hardly constitutes 'knowing who Aristotle is'.

Despite the unfortunate footnote in 'Über Sinn und Bedeutung' concerning the sense of proper names, Frege's more considered (and more defensible) position is expressed in the *Grundlagen*: 'Moreover, there is nothing contained in the name 'Columbus' about discovery or about America, even though it is the same man that we call Columbus and the discoverer of America.' (*Gl*.69.)

I can see no way to overcome the difficulties engendered by a negative answer to the question: 'Can one be said to know the sense of the sentence "Julius Caesar is dead" if one does not know who Julius Caesar is?'. And as the temptation to answer 'No' is not irresistible, we ought to examine the alternative.

In the first place an affirmative answer is not without its intuitive appeal. We would not say, for example, that a professor of Roman political history had a better understanding of the *sentence* 'Julius Caesar is dead' than a native speaker of English who knew nothing more about Julius Caesar than that he was a Roman general. Knowledge of facts about Julius Caesar is, in other words, of strictly limited relevance to the understanding of sentences which contain his name. Is it, then, of any relevance at all? The following considerations might seem to show that it is not. The opening sentence of D. H. Lawrence's short story *The Fox* is this: 'The two girls were usually known by their surnames, Banford and March'.[6] Now, native speakers of English do not react to this sentence with puzzlement; they have no difficulty in understanding its sense. And yet the sum total of our knowledge of the two girls is that they have the names 'Banford' and 'March', which (as Searle, Strawson, Kripke, and others have pointed out) is second only to knowing nothing about them whatsoever. This lack of knowledge has, however, no effect upon our understanding of the meaning of the sentence, which neither increases nor decreases as we read the rest of the story. This would seem to indicate that as long as we understand *that* a proper name is a proper name, we can understand any sentence in which it occurs. In response to the assertion 'Clara is arriving early tonight' I can reply with perfect propriety that I understand exactly what this sentence means, though I do not happen to know who Clara is. Indeed, my grasp of the meaning of the sentence is manifested, and not belied, by my saying in response 'I don't know who Clara is'.

[6] D. H. Lawrence, *The Short Novels*, vol. I, Chapter III, p. 3.

Now normally this response would be in order. But suppose that, in fact, 'Clara' is the name of a hurricane: it is then at least arguably the case that I have not understood the meaning of the sentence; that I have positively misunderstood it. (Generally speaking we can say that if a person has failed to understand a sentence his reaction will be one of puzzlement, whereas if he has misunderstood it his reaction will be an inappropriate one.) And if I respond to the news of the imminent arrival of Clara (the hurricane) by saying 'Oh good. Does she play bridge?' and by setting an extra place for dinner, then this is prima facie evidence for the conclusion that I have misunderstood the sentence in question.

If these observations are to the point, then a necessary condition of a person's being truly said to understand a proper name (or, better: to understand sentences containing that proper name) is that he knows what *sort* or *type* of object the name refers to.[7] The considerations adduced in the preceding paragraphs are, of course, inconclusive. They are intended to show merely that the conclusion reached is neither implausible nor recondite, conforming as it does to the things we would normally say about someone's use and understanding of proper names. None the less, such arguments from plausibility are here secondary to more directly philosophical considerations. For to accept the conclusion that the sense of a proper name is its referring to a determinate object of a given sort (or at least purporting to do so) is both to avoid the difficulties inherent in the barren Russellian notion of a logically proper name, and the difficulties inherent in the enriched notion of a proper name as shorthand for one or more definite descriptions. This leaves open, however, the possibility of accepting two important theses concerning proper names: we are free to accept with Frege that the *sense* of a proper name is usually indicated (but not stated) by identifying the *reference*, usually by employing a definite description; and with Strawson that it is a necessary condition for the possibility of our employing proper names at all that there be 'a backdrop of uniquely individuating descriptions' which pick out the object referred to by a name, independently of its being referred to by that name.[8] Neither of these theses entails that such descriptions are part of the *sense* of the proper name.

The force of Frege's analogy between a sentence and its truth-value,

---

[7] The notion of a sortal concept, to which tacit appeal is here made, is further elucidated below, Chapter II, §4.

[8] See P. F. Strawson, *Individuals*, Chapter 6.

and a proper name and its reference can now be elucidated. Just as one does not have to know whether a sentence is true or false in order to be able to understand it, so one does not need to know what object a name denotes in order to understand the sense of the name. And yet, (i) before one can be said to understand a sentence one must recognize that it is an expression which purports to be either-true-or-false (though one need not know which), so before one can be said to understand a proper name, one must recognize that it is an expression which purports to refer to an object of a certain sort (though one need not know to *which* object).[9] (ii) The concepts of truth-value and name-reference are linked in that a necessary (but not sufficient) condition for a sentence's being either true or false is that any proper name used therein should denote an object. As Frege observed, anyone who took a sentence of the form 'N.N is such and such' to be true (or false) would thereby be according a reference to the name 'N.N.'

To go this far with Frege does not, however, commit us to the further conclusion that the relation between a sentence and its truth-value is *the same* as that between a name and the object to which it refers. For while names are correlated conventionally with their references, sentences are manifestly not correlated conventionally with their truth-values.

The sense of a proper name, then, is that it purports to refer to a determinate object of a given sort with which it has been conventionally correlated. I understand the sense of 'Julius Caesar', say, when I know this: 'Julius Caesar' is a proper name of Julius Caesar, and Julius Caesar is a man. On this analysis, of course, it turns out that 'Julius Caesar is a man' is analytic; but this is a form of essentialism to which I have no objections. It will likewise be analytic that any given object falls under the sortal concept of largest scope under which it does in fact fall. Thus that 2 is a number, that love is an emotion, pain a sensation, Clara a hurricane, and Aristotle a man, all these will be analytic. (It will also be impossible that Aristotle was a hurricane, or 2 an emotion.) This incorporation of a sortal specification into the sense of a proper name has, as we shall see, very great advantages for the theory of functions.[10]

Now it might be argued that this move, which allows the analyticity

[9] The final substantiation of this point must await the distinction between input and output sense drawn below, Chapter IV, §3.

[10] See below, Chapter II, §6.

of the statement that Aristotle is a man, say, creates more difficulties than it solves. For if it is analytic that Aristotle is a man, and it follows that, therefore, something is a man, then this too must be analytic. But how, the objection runs, can it be analytic that there exists at least one man? Now this unacceptable consequence is avoided by denying that the move from

(4)   Aristotle is a man

to

(5)   Something is a man

is valid. And we are, in fact, committed to denying this by the fore-going theory of sense; for it was maintained that the sense of a proper name is that which one understands when one is able to use it correctly. And it is no part of one's understanding of a proper name that its purported bearer actually exists. It is part of the sense of such names as 'Aristotle', 'Pegasus', 'Odysseus', etc. that they *purport* to refer, but *not* that they actually succeed in referring. To deny this would commit us to one of two unacceptable consequences: either it would have to be denied that there can be an intelligible sentence which contains a vacuous proper name; or it would have to be asserted that all singular terms are successfully referential. Although it might be possible to lay down such rules for the manipulation of signs within a calculus, both alternatives are simply false with respect to the understanding we have of natural language. But in this case the move from (4) to (5) is as invalid, without the further premiss that Aristotle exists, as is the move from

(6)   Pegasus is a winged horse

to

(7)   Something is a winged horse.

In the posthumously published 'Dialog mit Pünjer über Existenz' Frege in fact asserts that 'from the proposition "Sachse is a man", the proposition "there are men" follows immediately' (*Nach*.67). Pünjer in reply argues, as I have done, that this is a *non sequitur* without the further premiss that Sachse exists. Frege replies: 'if "Sachse exists" is to mean "the word 'Sachse' is not an empty noise, but denotes something", then it is true that the condition "Sachse exists" must be fulfilled. This is no new premiss, however, but the obvious condition to which all our words conform.' (Ibid.) But this last observation is simply false: my dictionary tells me that Pegasus was a winged horse, but it does *not* imply that winged horses exist.

The dialogue with Pünjer dates from before 1884, that is long before Frege had distinguished the sense from the reference of an expression. This distinction, however, means that the dichotomy between an expression's being either 'an empty noise' or a sign which denotes something is not exhaustive, and cannot be used as Frege uses it in the last-quoted passage. Although standard contemporary logical calculi include a rule for existential generalization (warranting the move, e.g. from (4) to (5)) this is by no means as unavoidable or as uncontroversial as is sometimes made out. The stipulation that in a given calculus the rule of existential generalization shall be universally valid is tantamount to outlawing singular terms that have no reference. But this procedure is itself equivalent to allowing a suppressed existential premiss in any application of existential generalization. While there are practical justifications for allowing this premiss to remain suppressed in a given calculus, there is surely no philosophical justification for maintaining, as Frege did before 1884, that names which do not refer must be outlawed because they are semantically deviant.

5. SENTENCES AND INDIRECT DISCOURSE

The sense which an indicative sentence expresses Frege calls a Thought (*Gedanke*), and his most extended treatment of this notion is in the 1918 article of the same name. (I have indicated that 'Thought' is a technical term by writing it within an initial capital.) As Chapter IV below comprises a detailed and critical examination of the Fregean notion of a Thought, the present section will constitute merely the briefest introduction. The following, then, are some of the most important theses concerning Thoughts:

(i) Thoughts are objective. 'By a Thought I understand not the subjective performance of thinking but its objective content, which is capable of being the common property of several thinkers.' (*SuB*.32n.) Frege distinguishes the Thought, which is the truth-valuable component of a sentence's meaning, from the subjective contents of consciousness such as ideas, sensations, and images. 'We are not the bearers of Thoughts as we are the bearers of ideas.'

(*Ged.*74.) The aim of the sciences is to establish which Thoughts are true and which false; and Frege argues that such sciences as mathematics and physics, say, deal with an objective and impersonal realm of facts, and are not merely branches of psychology dealing with peoples' ideas about mathematics and physics respectively.

But not only are Thoughts, for Frege, objective entities in that their *existence* is not dependent upon their being grasped or thought by any person; they are also objective in that their internal make-up may contain only that which is in theory truth-valuable: 'I call a Thought something for which the question of truth arises.' (*Ged.*60.) In other words, the difference in meaning between the two sentences

<blockquote>Alas, John Smith has lost a leg</blockquote>

and

<blockquote>John Smith has lost a leg</blockquote>

do not concern the sense, the Thought expressed by the sentences.[11] 'What is called mood, fragrance, illumination in a poem, what is portrayed by cadence and rhythm, does not belong to the Thought.' (*Ged.*63.) Consequently Frege distinguishes between the *content* (*Inhalt*) of a sentence and the *Thought* (*Gedanke*) which it expresses: the content may include the Thought, along with other elements of the sentence's over-all meaning, for instance its connotations, emotive elements, presuppositions, emphases, and the like. 'Thus the contents of a sentence often go beyond the Thought expressed by it.' (*Ged.*63.)

(ii) *Thoughts are complete.* If the content of a sentence may extend further than the Thought expressed by it, it may also happen, as Frege points out, that a sentence possesses an intelligible content but yet expresses no Thought. Sentences which contain irreducible indexical and token-reflexive elements will be of this sort, as will those which contain a tensed verb without a precise time indication, or those which are too vague to possess a determinate truth-value. The sentence

<blockquote>I am drunk today</blockquote>

for example, does not express a Fregean Thought. In the first place, the personal pronoun only picks out a person when the sentence is considered along with its context of utterance. In everyday speech it is usually clear from the context of utterance who is the subject of an

[11] Cf. *Semantic Syntax*, ed. P. A. M. Seuren, p. 101.

assertion expressed by a sentence whose grammatical subject is a personal pronoun. But in such a case it is not the sentence, but the sentence along with its contextual determinants which expresses the Thought. Secondly, the above sentence fails to express a Thought because it contains no indication of the time of utterance; though again this is something that is usually supplied by the context in which it is spoken or written. 'If a time indication is needed by the present tense one must know when the sentence was uttered in order to apprehend the Thought correctly. Therefore the time of the utterance is part of the expression of the Thought.' (*Ged*.64.) Now if such indeterminacies are resolved, not by the context, but by explicit elements within the sentence, then the sentence itself, Frege believes, will express a Thought.[12] In the present case the sentence would have to be of the form:

I (so and so) am drunk today (the such and such, at time *t*).

But if all indeterminacies of sense are thus resolved internally, the *Thought expressed by this sentence* will possess a truth-value which may never change, regardless of who utters the sentence, or when, or into which language the sentence is translated, or what change of sense the words in it may undergo. Moreover the Thought expressed by this sentence would be true (or false) regardless of whether anyone ever uttered it, or entertained it. It is such considerations as these which lead Frege to assert that Thoughts are eternal and immutable, and that

(iii) *Thoughts are the primary bearers of truth-values*. 'When we say a sentence is true, we really mean its sense is.' For the moment we can ignore the more contentious aspects of this doctrine, and concentrate upon its plausible elements. Thus it is that, speaking common-sensically, truth (or falsity) is ascribed to what a person says, the statements that he makes, and not to the words or sentences which he uses. In certain circumstances, for instance, a person with a knowledge of a number of European languages would be able to express the Thought that it is raining by saying 'Il pleut', 'Es regnet', or 'It is raining'. The Thought (at least when completed by appropriate time and place indicators) would be the same in each case; and it would presumably be the speaker's intention to assert *this Thought* (rather than, say, utter just these words) in the belief that in so doing,

[12] But cf. below, Chapter IV, §3 where certain objections are levelled against this doctrine.

what he was asserting was true. Although there are limits to the amount of work that can be demanded of this vehicle/content model, the intuitions from which it springs are surely unexceptionable.

(iv) *Thoughts are unassertive.* In his early and middle-period works Frege identified a Thought with the truth-valuable meaning of an indicative sentence, and maintained that interrogative and imperative sentences expressed, not Thoughts, but questions and commands respectively. In the *Logische Untersuchungen,* however, he modified this doctrine so as to take account of the fact that certain questions can be answered either 'Yes' or 'No'. (Frege calls such questions propositional-questions, *Satzfragen.*) Such a question, Frege argues, must express a Thought—a Thought which an affirmative answer asserts to be true, and a negative answer, false. It is the Thought itself which is either true or false; but the Thought itself does not *say* whether it is true or false either as expressed by an indicative sentence or by a propositional question. For if it did, a propositional question would contain within itself its own answer. The Thought itself must therefore be without assertive force (cf. *Ged.*62; *Vern.*145; *Gef.*34). As Wittgenstein wrote in the *Tractatus,* where his use of the term proposition (*Satz*) corresponds closely to Frege's use of the term 'Thought': 'It is quite impossible for a proposition to state that it itself is true' (4.442). Wittgenstein directed this remark at both Frege and Russell; but in the former case at least the criticism is misplaced. For Frege maintained that assertive force must be clearly distinguished from the Thought expressed by a sentence, and introduced the special sign '⊢———' in order to indicate when assertive force was present. But while this force attaches to the Thought, it is, *pace* Wittgenstein, no part of the Thought. If it were, all propositional questions would be begged.

(v) *Normal and indirect sense must be distinguished.* The four theses examined above concern what Frege called the normal sense (*Gewöhnlicher Sinn*) of an indicative sentence or propositional question. The two sentences 'Julius Caesar is dead' and 'Is Julius Caesar dead?' both, as they stand, express the same Thought; and the former refers to its truth-value. There are certain contexts and constructions which, however, will alter this state of affairs: quotation, for example: 'In direct quotation a sentence designates another sentence, and in indirect quotation a Thought' (*SuB.*36).

If words are used in the ordinary way, what one intends to speak of is their reference. It can also happen, however, that one wishes to speak about the words themselves, or about their sense. This happens, for instance, when the words of another are (directly) quoted. One's words then first designate words of the other speaker, and only the latter have their normal reference. . . . In reported speech one talks about the sense of another person's remarks . . . In reported speech words are used *indirectly* or have their indirect reference. We distinguish accordingly the normal reference from the indirect reference of a word; and its normal from its indirect sense. The indirect reference of a word is accordingly its normal sense. (*SuB*.28.)

In other words, if I utter the sentence 'Julius Caesar is dead' in a normal conversational situation, the words which I utter have their normal sense and reference: 'Julius Caesar' refers to the man of that name, and the sentence as a whole expresses the Thought that Julius Caesar is dead, and refers to the True. But if I now say that the sentence 'Julius Caesar is dead' occurs in the preceding sentence on this page, then the words in the last quoted sentence refer to *words* in the previous sentence. And finally, if I say 'Shakespeare said that Julius Caesar is dead', the subordinate clause 'that Caesar is dead' refers to the *sense* of the sentence 'Julius Caesar is dead', i.e. to the Thought thus expressed. And so, for Frege, in ascribing a statement or a belief to someone, I neither refer to the words (if any) which he uttered or entertained, nor to the truth-value (if any) of what he asserted or believed, but only to the Thought which he expressed or entertained.

6. FUNCTIONS

After the lengthy digression of the last three sections we can now return to the problem which constitutes the primary subject-matter of the present chapter: Can a more satisfactory account of predicates and predication be provided by employing the notion of unsaturatedness of sense than was possible, following Frege, by appeal to the notion of reference?

P. F. Strawson has summarized the Kantian thesis that 'Thoughts without content are empty and intuitions without concepts are blind' (*B*.75) as follows: 'The duality of intuitions and concepts is, in fact, just one form or aspect of a duality which must be recognized in any philosophy which is seriously concerned with human knowledge, its objects, or its expression and communication.'[13] Within the latter

---

[13] P. F. Strawson, *The Bounds of Sense*, p. 47.

realm of expression and communication, Strawson adds, 'we must recognize the need for such linguistic or other devices as will enable us both to classify or describe in general terms and to indicate to what particular cases our classifications or descriptions are being applied.' Now, although Kant was primarily exercised by the problem of establishing and clarifying this duality within an epistemological context, there is an important strand in Kantian thought with which Frege would have been in full accord: that experience is 'anything to us' depends upon our ability to subsume objects under concepts. And this ability is both manifest in and dependent upon our ability to formulate and express assertoric judgements: 'The *only* use which the understanding can make of concepts is to *judge* by means of them' (*B*.93). It is this thesis which justifies the use which Kant makes of the traditional classification of the 'functions of judgement' as the means of isolating and identifying those concepts which are necessary to our having the experiences we do have. But what Kant endeavoured to establish by appeal to the Table of Judgements, Frege attempted by appeal to the semantic and syntactic properties of the expressions we use in formulating judgements. Frege, indeed, translated the transcendental-psychological investigation of Kant into a semantico-ontological one. Which is to say that where Kant urges the absolute irreducibility of *intuitions* and *concepts*, but yet the necessity of their co-operation in any possible human experience, Frege urges the absolute irreducibility of *objects* and *concepts* (or functions), and of proper names and functional signs, but yet maintains that no meaningful Thought can be formulated without the participation within it of elements corresponding to both types. And for both philosophers the reason is the same: if this were not the case then thoughts would not possess the unity or completeness which is their essential and defining characteristic. 'By a "function"', wrote Kant, 'I mean the unity of the act of bringing various representations under one representation.' (*B*.93.) Frege makes much the same point in the following passages, albeit in a somewhat different terminology. I have quoted these passages in full, in order to combat the widespread, almost universally held belief amongst critics of, and commentators on, Frege that he nowhere explicitly deals with, or even hints at the unsaturatedness of functional *sense*.[14] The following passages show that not only did Frege maintain that predicates and other expressions

[14] e.g. W. Marshall, 'Frege's Theory of Functions and Objects', and R. Grossmann, 'Frege's Ontology'.

possess a sense as well as a reference (this has been doubted[15]), but also that *both* are essentially incomplete, and, moreover, it is predicate *sense* that is the prior, more basic concept:

Statements in general . . . can be imagined to be split up into two parts; one complete in itself, and the other in need of supplementation or 'unsaturated'. Thus, e.g. we split up the sentence

'Caesar conquered Gaul'

into 'Caesar' and 'conquered Gaul'. The second part is 'unsaturated'—it contains an empty place; only when this place is filled up with a proper name *does a complete sense appear.* (*FuB*.17, my italics.)

If then we look upon *Thoughts* as composed of simple parts and take these, in turn, to correspond to the simple parts of sentences . . . the question now arises how the Thought comes to be constructed, and how its parts are so combined together that the whole amounts to something more than the parts taken separately. . . . The whole owes its unity to the fact that the Thought saturates the unsaturated part or, as we might also say, completes the part in need of completion. . . . A Thought is saturated and needs no completion. (*Gef*.36–7, my italics.)

The words 'unsaturated' and 'predicative' seem to suit the sense better than the reference . . . (*ASB*. in *Nach*.129.)

Frege did, of course, on many occasions allude to the incompleteness of predicate reference, of the concept. But what has gone entirely unnoticed is that he justified this doctrine by appeal to the prior notion of the unsaturatedness of predicate sense. And this is nowhere clearer than in the following passage, where, having stated that objects and concepts (references) must be absolutely distinguished, he then justifies this claim as follows:

For not all the parts of a Thought may be complete; at least one must be 'unsaturated' or predicative; otherwise they would not hold together. For example, the sense of the phrase 'the number 2' does not hold together with that of the expression 'the concept *prime number*' without a link. We apply such a link in the sentence 'the number 2 falls under the concept *prime number*'; the link is contained in the words 'falls under' which need to be completed in two ways: by a subject and an accusative. And only because their sense is unsaturated are they capable of serving as a link. Only when they have been supplemented is this twofold respect do we get a complete sense, a Thought. (*BuG*.205.)

[15] W. Marshall, 'Sense and Reference: a Reply'.

For Frege, then, it is in the realm of sense—that is, in connection with the unity of Thought—that the irreducible difference between objects and concepts must ultimately be located. And this is to be expected; for if we take a sentence like 'Sherlock Holmes was fat', which contains a proper name *and* a predicate which have no reference (the former because there is no such person as Sherlock Holmes; the latter because '( ) was fat' contains no time specification and is not defined for all objects), the considerations advanced by Frege still apply with all their force.

At this point we can take up again the question of predicate reference from where we left it at the end of Chapter I. We argued that Frege had not one, but two notions of reference: the transitive notion, whereby having a reference involves being correlated with some extra-linguistic entity; and the intransitive notion, whereby referring involves no more than possessing some (unspecified) property in virtue of which the expression in question could participate in sentences possessing a determinate truth-value. This latter we called the property of being truth-valuable. It was argued, further, that Frege's account of what it is for a predicate to be truth-valuable, namely its being defined for any object whatever as argument, is mistaken—at least if it is intended to apply to the language of common discourse. But what of the claim that predicates refer transitively, i.e. that, besides expressing a sense, a predicate also refers to a concept, on the model which Frege presented in his letter to Husserl (Fig. 5)?

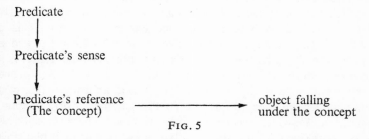

Predicate

↓

Predicate's sense

↓

Predicate's reference ⟶ object falling
(The concept) under the concept

FIG. 5

Frege immediately adds: 'I have written the last step from concept to object sideways in order to indicate that it belongs to the same level, that concepts and objects *have the same objectivity*.' (*Brief.* 96, my italics.) Frege, like many philosophers concerned with the foundations of science and mathematics, sought to protect objectivity in science by grounding his basic categories *ontologically*, by adopting, that is, an extreme form of platonic realism. So it is that not only concrete objects, but abstract objects, concepts, functions, senses, and truth-values are accorded ontological status as a means of protecting their objectivity against the pernicious encroachment of philosophical idealism and scientific psychologism. We have already seen that Frege's programme breaks down when applied to the language of ordinary discourse: it places intolerably narrow constraints upon what expressions are to be passed as semantically fit; and it produces ontologically unacceptable (if intelligible) results, such as a truth-value's being an object composed of a complete and an incomplete part. Frege's mature works contain no indication that he ever considered that there might be any philosophically acceptable alternative to an indiscriminate platonism as a means of guaranteeing the objectivity of logic, mathematics, and science. (Even though his early *Habilitationsschrift* is essentially constructivistic, and his late, posthumously published remarks on number are Kantian.) Frege generally saw the abandonment of platonism as a capitulation to psychologism, which he believed would 'end in truth being reduced to individuals' taking something to be true' (*Gg.*xv). I shall try to show that there is no reason why we should follow Frege here.

We asked earlier: What useful work does the Fregean notion of a concept, the transitive reference of a predicate, perform? And the answer is, surely, none. We can see this is the case by asking: What would it be like for a predicate to *lack* a reference, even though it expressed a clear sense? This would involve the predicate's being able to participate in sentences expressing a clear and univocal Thought, but which could not have a truth-value, either true or false. This, as we have seen, is a conceivable state of affairs with respect to proper names (like 'Odysseus') which have a sense but lack a reference. Is it, however, conceivable with respect to predicates? If 'a' is a proper name which successfully refers, and '$\phi(\ )$' is a predicate with a clear sense, under what conditions would the sentence '$\phi(a)$' express a sense, but one which was neither true nor false? There are only two types of case in which this state of affairs is even prima facie plausible: (i) the case in which, although '$\phi(\ )$' has a clear sense for a certain range of objects as arguments, it is not defined for objects of the category to which a belongs. For example, '$\phi(\ )$' might be '( ) is prime', and 'a' might be a non-numerical name, say, 'Aristotle'. (ii) There is the case in which the predicate itself contains a proper name which lacks a reference, as does, for instance, the predicate '( ) is a brother of Odysseus' or '( ) saw a moon of Vulcan'.

In cases of type (ii), it follows from the Fregean principle for the determination of reference, *PR1*, that any sentence which contains the predicate '( ) saw a moon of Vulcan' will be without a truth-value; for such a sentence will contain a proper name which lacks a reference: 'Vulcan'. But suppose, for example, a philosopher-astronomer, say, Hegel, claims in seriousness to have sighted one of the moons of Vulcan. Our reaction would be that he is mistaken, that what he says is false. For there *is* no planet Vulcan, and hence no moons of Vulcan which can be seen. And if it is impossible to do something, then any claim to have succeeded in doing that thing must be false. And, contrarywise, the sentence

It is not the case that Hegel saw a moon of Vulcan

is *true*.[16]

In cases like (i), in which the predicate has a clear sense but is completed by a name of an object belonging to a category to which the predicate does not apply, again, Frege's theory yields the most implausible results. If *any* sentence in which the predicate '( ) is a prime number' occurs is to have a truth-value, then every sentence in which it occurs must have a truth-value (assuming that the name which occurs in the argument-place has a reference). But here are included such sentences as 'Aristotle is a prime number', 'The square root of Aristotle is a prime number', 'The steam from my porridge plus the square root of Aristotle is a prime number', and so on. We noted above (Chapter I, section 6) that there are insuperable difficulties facing any attempt either to construe such nonsensical sentences as possessing a truth-value in virtue of the sense(?) which they express, or to stipulate a truth-value for them *ad hoc*. Now, the account we have given of the notion of sense as it applies to proper names (Chapter II, section 4) can be employed to construct a more feasible theory. The sense of a proper name contains a stipulation or indication of the category of object to which it refers. In other words, anyone who understands or knows how to use a given proper name thereby knows at least one sortal concept under which the object to which it refers falls. A sortal concept is a concept which tells us what

---

[16] In case it is thought that this argument somehow depends upon the intentionality of the verb 'to see' in '( ) saw a moon of Vulcan', it ought to be pointed out that the argument goes through if the non-intentional predicate '( ) is a brother of Odysseus' is substituted, *mutatis mutandis*, throughout.

sort or type of thing an object is; more precisely, a sortal concept provides us with an independent principle of counting.[17] In Strawson's words: 'A sortal [concept] supplies a principle for distinguishing and counting individual particulars which presupposes no antecedent principle, or method, of individuating the particulars it collects.' (*Individuals*, 168–9.) Such concepts as *man, number, word, sensation,* or (moment in) *time* are sortal concepts; *wise, prime, efficient, English,* and *old*, on the other hand, are not. I shall call such non-sortal concepts attributive. As Strawson has remarked, attributive concepts, even though they may supply 'principles of grouping, even of counting, particulars, supply such principles only for particulars already distinguished or distinguishable, in accordance with some antecedent principle or method' (ibid.). The suggestion advanced in Chapter II, section 4, then, boils down to this: the only concept or concepts which we necessarily know an object to fall under when we know the sense of that object's name are pure sortal concepts. I say 'pure' because, of course, there are sortal concepts which contain explicit attributive elements. One can, for example, individuate and count bald left-handed men, and *bald left-handed man* is technically a sortal concept. It is, however, a mixed sortal, containing within it, besides the pure sortal concept *man*, the attributive elements *bald* and *left-handed*. And so, to understand the meaning of a sentence in which the name 'Aristotle' is used, I must at least know one pure sortal concept under which Aristotle falls; I do *not* need to know, of any attributive concept, whether or not Aristotle falls under it. This means that I need to know rather little about Aristotle in order to understand sentences in which his name occurs; but then names *are* rather uninformative.

Our contention, then, is this: a name manifests, through its sense, a certain *sortal physiognomy*, which is recognized by anyone who knows how to use that name. Now, if it can be shown that (again metaphorically) the argument-place in a predicate also possesses a similar sortal physiognomy, determined by its sense, then we shall have the beginnings of a model of sentence sense which will clearly outlaw such inappropriate acts of predication as those instanced above (type (i)).

But before proceeding to the defence of a particular theory of predicate sense, it will be as well if we pause briefly here and ask: What is to be expected of such a theory; what requirements ought it

[17] In addition to the work of Strawson, cf. also D. Wiggins, *Identity and Spatio-Temporal Continuity*, pp. 1–3.

to fulfil? Sense, we have already said, is a notion needed in epistemology, in order to explain how we learn, understand, and communicate by means of language. So our account must conform to the phenomenological data with which we, as native language users, are fully familiar concerning what it is to understand a predicate, or an act of predication, or a sentence in which a given predicate is used. Secondly, as a basically Fregean position is being defended here, we must endeavour to provide an interpretation and justification of his doctrine that concepts are a form of *function*, and that functions are essentially *unsaturated*. We must also show, thirdly, that this theory is possible and plausible in the absence of Frege's notion of predicate *reference*. Fourthly, we need an account of what is amiss with such sentences as 'Green ideas sleep furiously' and 'Three was the colour of the pain in my chair', where the predicates are clearly not defined for all objects as arguments, and where, as a result, Frege's theory does not apply. And finally, our account of predicate sense must combine with that provided above of the sense of proper names, so as to constitute at least the bare bones of a theory of sentence sense, of the Thought.

What, then, is the sense of a predicate? Given the preceding accounts of what sense in general is, and of what a predicate is, this question is tantamount to asking: When a person understands a sentence, say: 'A is drunk', what is it that he understands that will enable him also and therewith to understand the sentences 'B is drunk', 'C is drunk', and so on? What does that person know when he knows how to use the predicate '( ) is drunk'? The answer towards which we are working is that such a person knows a rule or principle for the collection of objects of a certain sort of type. Although this is an answer that is not without its contentious and philosophical aspects, we can treat it for the moment as simply an attempt to embody this uncontrovertible observation: If someone is unable to identify or pick out drunken beings, if he repeatedly predicates '( ) is drunk' of sober individuals, or of objects which are of the wrong type (e.g. trees, tables, and clouds), then that person would not be said to understand what the predicate '( ) is drunk' means. And this is true even should the person be able to define the predicate by saying it means 'being intoxicated or under the influence of alcohol'. For if he then persisted in making either predominantly false, or predominantly inappropriate judgements of drunkenness, this would merely show that he did not understand the definition either.

A person's ability to formulate appropriate and largely true judgements employing a given concept is a more basic criterion for the ascription to him of a grasp of that concept, than an ability to define, or *say* what that concept means. This is especially clear in the case of these concepts which, like colour concepts, cannot be defined verbally.

But in what way are we now using the word 'concept'? We have argued that the Fregean notion of a concept (as the reference of a predicate) is, if not actually mistaken, then at least otiose. Is there, then, a more respectable use for the term? It was employed in the last paragraph as synonymous with the *sense of a predicate*; and it is thus that it will be employed henceforward, for the remainder of the present work.

The provisional result of the investigation thus far is that a concept is what a predicate expresses, the sense of a predicate; and this has been glossed as being *a rule for the collection of objects of a certain sort or type*. A person's grasp of such a rule will be manifest in his ability to pick out objects to which the predicate applies; and one, but by no means the only way of doing this is by asserting true judgements about such objects. That is, picking out the objects in language, by *referring* to them, and asserting truly that they fall under the concept in question.

All this sounds rather un-Fregean. And the reason is that we have introduced what might be called a *transcendental* element into our account. Frege's approach, by contrast, was essentially *mundane*. Frege, that is, extrapolated immediately and directly from the nature of language, from facts about syntax and semantics, to the nature of the world. This sometimes has the most startling results; for example when he observes that 'a statement does not contain an empty place, and therefore we must regard what it stands for as an object' (*FuB.* 18); or when he posits the existence of 'unsaturated' entities to correspond to incomplete expressions (*Funk.*665). Typically Frege ascribes a reference, in some ontological realm, to *all* semantically primitive elements: proper names, predicates and functional signs, sentences, subordinate clauses, and even logical connectives. And such elements are isolated by considering possibilities of substitution *salva veritate* and *salva congruitate*. In this general approach Frege has set the tone, the aims, and the methods of virtually all subsequent work in philosophical logic and semantics, at least in the English-speaking world. Russell and the early Wittgenstein, and later Quine, Tarski, Carnap, Church, and Davidson, with only minor deviations, have trod the Fregean path. The major exception has been the author of the *Philosophical Investigations* (though one ought to mention here those, like Grice and Strawson, who have been strongly influenced by him).[18] Wittgenstein realized in his later work that only a transcendental approach to the study of language is able to establish conclusions of the type in which we are here interested. And he showed that such an approach must needs assume that there is a community of language users whose linguistic activities are not cut off from other, non-linguistic habits, customs, and activities. Language, Wittgenstein maintained, is not a formal calculus but a human tool whose construction and function become incomprehensible when it is divorced from the 'forms of life' in which it is used. It is indeed precisely in order to restore the notion of a language to the context in which it belongs, from which it has been removed by philosophers, and wherein only it can be adequately understood, that Wittgenstein introduces the notion of a 'language-*game*'.

Hintikka has recently complained that the 'transcendental point of view', which concentrates upon the human activities essentially involved in our obtaining whatever information we have, 'is notoriously absent from recent philosophising'. And although he claims he is not overlooking the 'rich Wittgensteinian literature on "language-games"' yet feels that 'the study of the relations of our language . . . to the reality which it speaks of has either been left unattended, or else has been discussed only in terms of unanalysed "interpretations", "valuations" . . . or comparable unanalysed static ties between language and the world, . . . even though it is obvious that these are not natural relations but are only created by and sustained through certain human activities and human institutions.'[19] One can only agree. And the responsibility for this neglect lies, more than with any other single philosopher, with Gottlob Frege. The point is not, however, that Frege's conclusions were false, or his method misconceived; on the contrary, it was because his method was so apt and his conclusions, on the whole, so correct that this deficiency passed unnoticed for so long. And the deficiency is this: what I am calling the 'mundane' methodology is insufficiently powerful to establish the conclusions which Frege wished about, say, concepts, judgement, numbers, and so on. One cannot establish that numbers are objects, for example, solely on the basis of the fact that

---

[18] Cf. Strawson's remarks on this topic in *Meaning and Truth*, pp. 4–5.
[19] J. Hintikka, *Logic, Language-Games and Information*, p. 99.

numerals are singular terms, or that a true sentence is the name of an object simply because it does not have an argument-place. Moreover the weakness of the method of immediate extrapolation from language to ontology is noted by Frege on many occasions: 'I can here only give hints', 'and here a metaphorical account must suffice', 'the reader must agree to meet me half way' and 'not begrudge a pinch of salt'.

In fact, the foregoing disclaimers were all issued in connection with the topic in hand, namely the nature of concepts and predicates, where the method of examining possibilities of substitution *salva veritate* and *salva congruitate* is conspicuously inadequate for the establishment of the conclusions Frege desires. If I have understood him aright, it is a transcendental element which Dummett is attempting to introduce into the following account of why Frege is right to deny that a concept and an object (a concept-correlate[20]) can be one and the same thing. Contesting the un-Fregean assertion that the two expressions 'the relation of difference' and '( ) is different from ( )' can stand for the same thing, Dummett writes: 'We cannot say this, because we come by the notion of a relation via the distinction between relational expressions and others, and 'the relation of difference' is not a relational expression. A relation, that is, is *explained* as being that for which a relational expression stands, and hence if we allow that an expression of a different kind can stand for a relation, the whole explanation of what a relation is falls to the ground.'[21] This is rather obscure, and just as it stands is, I believe, false (though this may be merely the result of an unfortunate choice of words on Dummett's part). What a relation is, Dummett says, is *explained* as that for which a relational expression stands; and likewise for concepts with respect to predicates. This is the way in which they are introduced to us. This seems to be right. But it hardly entails that, once introduced, once explained, there can subsequently be no alternative way of referring to a relation, without, that is, imperilling the original explanation. The possibility of the subsequent employment of a non-relational expression to refer to a relation surely does not entail the demise of 'the whole explanation of what a relation is'.

[20] 'Concept correlate' is Wells's term for the type of object which a nominalized predicate (e.g. 'drunkenness') denotes. See R. S. Wells, 'Frege's Ontology'. (Cf. *BuG*.197-8, *G&B*.46-7.)
[21] M. A. E. Dummett, 'Frege on Functions; a Reply', reprinted in *Klemke*,282.

But there is an ambiguity here; and this means that there are *two* problems of 'explaining what a relation is'. One is the problem of explaining what a relation is *per se* (i.e. as distinct from an object or a concept or an event, say); the other is the problem of explaining what a particular, but as yet unspecified relation is (e.g. the relation of *difference*). Let us call explanations of the former type *generic* explanations, and those of the latter type, *specific*. The specific case is of interest to philosophy, if at all, only in so far as that any generic explanation must not run counter to the specific ways in which relations are actually introduced and explained. But it is just this which Dummett seems to do. There is no reason why one could not introduce a specific relation by means of entirely non-relational expressions. But of course it is possible to do this only if one already has the generic notion of a relation. And it is this latter than cannot possibly be introduced or explained by any other means than via the common properties of relational expressions. And relational expressions are themselves abstractions from sentences.[22] If a semantic model is to be adequate to the language we speak, then it must allow that that language is accessible to human beings, that it is learnable. The nature and function of concepts and relations in human thought and communication cannot be divorced from our ability to apply them, with a considerable degree of success, to the objects we encounter. This ability is manifest in the making of true assertions, in the uttering of true sentences; and this is something we learn to do.

But does not this constitute a rejection, lock, stock, and barrel, of the Fregean notion of a concept? I do not think so. On the contrary, it constitutes a reinterpretation of the notion of unsaturatedness, a reaffirmation of the Fregean account of what a predicate is, and a development, along Fregean lines, of the notion of sense as it applies to incomplete expressions. This, it is true, nullifies Frege's platonism, according to which there exists something to which a predicate stands in the same relation as a proper name stands to its bearer; but it leaves the most important of Frege's insights intact, indeed, reinforced.

The concept is essentially predicative. A name of an object, on the other hand, is quite incapable of being used as a grammatical predicate. (*BuG*.193.)

Concept-words must possess a sense . . . otherwise they are just an empty series of sounds. (*ASB*. in *Nach*. 136.)

[22] See above, Chapter I, §5.

With this we can agree, if we add that (i) a univocal sense is all that a predicate need possess in order to be truth-valuable, and (ii) this notion of sense is one that cannot be divorced from the other linguistic activities of a community of language users. But this is, precisely, to interpret Frege's insight that a predicate results from the deletion of a singular term from an *assertive* sentence, from a transcendental point of view. Before we turn to an explicit examination of the transcendental aspects of the notion of *sense*, however, we must pause to consider certain problems associated with the nature of *assertion*.

CHAPTER III

ASSERTION

THE purpose of the present chapter is to examine the notion of *assertion* or *assertive force:* to examine critically Frege's theory concerning this, and to establish an account that will constitute a useful element in our analysis of judgement.

1. THE *BEGRIFFSSCHRIFT*

In section 3 of Chapter I, we to some extent anticipated the concerns of the present chapter when we subjected Frege's use of the two concept-script signs '⊢————' and '————' to a brief scrutiny. We there, however, examined only his use of these signs in the *Grundgesetze* of 1893. To understand Frege's theory fully we must now return to his first published work, the *Begriffsschrift* of 1879, and to the first doctrine propounded in that work:

A judgement is always to be expressed by means of the sign

⊢————

This stands to the left of the sign or complex of signs in which the content of the judgement is given. (*Bs*.1.)

And a few lines later he specifies that

As a constituent of the sign ⊢———— the horizontal stroke combines the symbols following into a whole; assertion, which is expressed by the vertical stroke, relates to the whole thus formed. (*Bs*.2.)

Already, then, a number of important distinctions have been introduced with a disconcerting brevity. On the one hand there is the representation, as it appears in the concept-script, of a complete judgement that something is the case:

(a)   ⊢———— *Δ*

If the vertical stroke to the left of this complex is omitted, there remains the symbol

(b)   ———— *Δ*

which, Frege tells us, represents 'a thought', 'a proposition', or 'a mere complex of ideas'. If (a) represents the judgement that 'unlike magnetic poles attract one another', Frege says, then the sign '——— $\varDelta$', 'will *not* express this judgement; it will be intended merely to produce in the reader the idea of the mutual attraction of unlike magnetic poles' (*Bs*.2). Finally, there is the sign

(c) $\varDelta$

which represents the 'conceptual content' of (a) and (b). '$\varDelta$' must always represent a 'possible content of judgement'; it cannot, therefore, represent an object or, indeed, anything that is not fundamentally sentential or propositional.

In the opening sections of the *Begriffsschrift*, then, Frege establishes the following terminology, to which I shall endeavour to adhere, at least until something more appropriate can be established: (a) represents a *judgement*; (b) represents a *proposition*; (c) represents a *conceptual content* of a possible judgement. The sign '|———' is called the *judgement sign*, and it is composed of two parts: the horizontal or *content stroke*, and the vertical *assertion stroke*.

So much, then, for the broad outlines of what is surely a somewhat recondite series of distinctions. Why, we might well ask, did Frege think it so important to have the difference (whatever it might exactly be) between asserted and unasserted contents of judgement clearly marked in the concept-script? The distinction is one that went unmarked in the history of logic before Frege; and it has gone largely unmarked since.[1] Presumably, however, Frege thought that to overlook this distinction would be to jeopardize the validity of proofs formulated within the concept-script: 'In my formalized language . . . only that part of judgements which affects possible inferences is taken into consideration. Whatever is needed for valid inference is fully expressed; what is not needed is for the most part not indicated either; no scope is left for conjecture.' (*Bs*.3.) In what way, then, would the validity of inference be vitiated or threatened by a failure to be clear about the presence or absence of assertive force? This is

---

[1] So far as I am aware there exist only two detailed treatments of the notion of *assertion* published in English: P. T. Geach, 'Assertion', *Phil. Rev.* lxxiv (1965), 448–54; M. A. E. Dummett, *Frege: Philosophy of Language*, Chapter 10. Although the sign '|———' has passed into general usage, it is not today employed with the meaning which Frege attached to it. It is now construed as a unitary symbol which indicates that what follows it is a theorem, provable in a given system.

one question which we must answer. Another, more basic one is this: just *what* did Frege think that assertive force was, and *to what* did he think it attached? Roughly speaking, the answers to these questions will be as follows. On the one hand, Frege's intuitions concerning the role of assertion in inference are well founded: assertive force is something which can and does affect the validity of proofs. On the other hand, however, Frege was confused about the nature of this force; sometimes he thought it a psychological phenomenon attaching to mental acts; and sometimes a purely logical matter concerning the position of propositions within a proof; and, yet again, a matter of syntax concerning the difference between a sentence and the corresponding nominalization. But even here Frege's intuitions are not untoward; for the two signs '———' and '|———' *can* be used to mark important distinctions in all these areas. Frege was to write in the *Grundgesetze* that

the same thing may never be defined twice, because it would then remain in doubt whether these definitions were consistent with one another. (*Gg*.§33.)

Now although Frege nowhere in the *Bergiffsschrift* defines the terms 'proposition', 'judgement', or 'assertion', or the signs '———' or '|———', exactly the same point can be made about the partial explanations which he there offers: it is not clear whether they are consistent with one another. To these explanations I now turn.

2. A BOGUS DISTINCTION

One of the distinctions considered essential by most traditional theories of judgement was that between the subject and the predicate of a judgement. This distinction, Frege tells us somewhat surprisingly 'finds *no place* in my way of representing a judgement' (*Bs*.2). What Frege means here, however, is not that he repudiates in its entirety any distinction between subject and predicate, but rather that he rejects one, traditional, way of representing this distinction.

The Greek capital '*Δ*', we have said, is to represent the conceptual content of a judgement; and some idea of what this latter is, is provided by Frege's remark that the following two sentences have the same conceptual content: 'The Greeks defeated the Persians at Plataea' and 'The Persians were defeated by the Greeks at Plataea'. The criterion for ascribing sameness of conceptual content here is that 'all inferences which can be drawn from the first judgement when combined with other ones can be drawn from the second when combined with the same other judgements' (*Bs*.3). Clearly, then, the difference between the two sentences, which consists primarily in a difference in subject/predicate construction, is logically immaterial and would not be represented in a perspicuous notation. What it is that the two sentences express can, without equivocation, be represented by the single sign '*Δ*'. Now here, I believe, long before the introduction of the distinction between sense and reference we can witness the first emergence of a train of thought which was eventually to lead to the construing of sentences as a species of *name*, referring to their truth-values. For, having decided to symbolize the conceptual content of a judgement in a way which transcends internal subject/ predicate analysis, *Frege feels compelled to introduce a predicate of which this conceptual content itself is the subject*. Already '*Δ*' is beginning to look rather like a singular term! The predicate which Frege then introduces is none other than the sign '⊢———':

Our symbolic language is a language of this sort: the symbol ⊢——— is the common predicate of all judgements . . . Such a language would have only a single predicate, viz: 'is a fact'. (*Bs*.4)

In other words, ordinary judgements of the form: *S is P* will be translated into those of the form: *that S is P is a fact*. Such, then, is the role of the sign '⊢———' in the concept-script. It is to be the 'common predicate of all judgements'.

There is virtually nothing to be said in favour of this theory. In the first place, it is quite redundant and introduces neither precision nor perspicuity. Frege has already stipulated that '*Δ*' is to stand only for a possible content of judgement, i.e. for something whose form is *already* propositional. He then, however, introduces the operator '———' which turns sentences into their nominalizations (i.e. turns '*p*' into 'that *p*') and feels compelled to introduce another operator, the vertical stroke, which will turn the nominalization back into a sentence (i.e. turns 'that *p*' into 'it is a fact that *p*'). Quite apart from the fact that this whole manœuvre is redundant, it is philosophically pernicious; for it makes it appear (a) that assertive force belongs to the predicate in a judgement, and (b) that the unity of a judgement is the same as, or closely analogous to, the unity of a complex *name*. (The operator '———' which is supposed to bind the symbols which follow it into a whole which can then be asserted is, precisely, a *nominalizing* operator.) But (a) cannot be the case, for *any* predicate which is supposed to embody assertive force can occur in a context which necessarily robs it of that force: for example, when it occurs as the predicate in the antecedent of a conditional proposition. The falsity of (b) is harder to establish, and much of what follows will be directed to this end. As we shall see, Frege very quickly rejected (a) outright; (b) on the other hand was eventually to be embraced in an even stronger form than in the *Begriffsschrift*.

3. A LOGICAL DISTINCTION

The judgement sign can only occur at the beginning, that is to the left of a sign or complex of signs representing a conceptual content. The vertical stroke which comprises one of its two parts signifies the presence of assertive force. These two characteristics enable the judgement stroke to mark a valid and important distinction: between assertive and unassertive occurrences of one and the same proposition.

In the following inference schema (*modus ponens*), the propositional variable '*p*' occurs twice:

(i)   If *p* then *q*

(ii)   But *p*,

(iii) Therefore *q*.

Now, roughly speaking to begin with, there is a sense in which both occurrences of '*p*' must stand for *one and the same thing:* otherwise the argument is vitiated by equivocation. On the other hand, however, there must be a sense in which the two occurrences of '*p*' are quite different: if '*p*' in (i) is assertive, then premiss (ii) is redundant; but if '*p*' in (ii) is not assertive, then the argument will not go through.

Russell seems to have grasped just half of this argument in the following passage from *The Principles of Mathematics:*

It is plain that, if I may be allowed to use the word *assertion* in a non-psychological sense, the proposition '*p* implies *q*' *asserts* an implication, though it does not *assert p* or *q*. (*PMs*.35.)

This is quite right; but then, inexplicably, Russell goes on to add that

The *p* and *q* which enter into this proposition are not strictly the same as the *p* and *q* which are separate propositions, at least if they are true. (Ibid.)

Now this would imply that either all inferences of the form *modus ponens* (to take but one example) are invalid, or, at least, that all those with either a true antecedent or a true consequent in the conditional premiss are invalid. This is, of course, quite unacceptable.

Let us examine first the occurrence of 'p' in premiss (i). It will be admitted that there is a marked difference in the truth-conditions between sentences of the form 'If p then q' and those of the form 'Because p, therefore q'. If someone were to utter the sentence 'Because it is raining, (therefore) you will stay indoors', he would be understood as having asserted that it *is* raining, and hence that the person addressed *will* stay indoors. This stands in contrast to the utterance of the sentence 'If it is raining, then you will stay indoors', in which neither the antecedent nor the consequent is asserted. In other words, 'Because p, therefore q; and not-p' is a contradiction. 'If p then q; and not-p' is not. Our grounds for saying that 'p' is not assertive as it occurs in the antecedent (or the consequent) of a hypothetical proposition are (a) it cannot be exported, and (b) the conjunction of 'not-p' to the hypothetical proposition does not yield a contradiction. In both these cases an 'If . . . then . . .' sentence stands contrasted with one of the form 'Because . . . therefore . . . '. And it is precisely because 'p' is unasserted in premiss (i), that premiss (ii) is needed; for premiss (ii) simply asserts that p is true.

The upshot of this is that we are compelled to recognize that *one and the same* proposition may occur now assertively, now unassertively. Geach has called this 'the Frege point', and seems to consider it the only point of substance which can be extracted from Frege's analysis of assertion, of his use of the judgement sign.[2] As we shall see, there are indeed other 'Frege points', but this is not to deny either the validity or the importance of this one.

But perhaps it will be argued that, inescapable though the distinction made here undoubtedly is, it is surely so obvious and incontrovertible as hardly to warrant the space here devoted to it. Yet the list of philosophers who have denied it is long and distinguished, and includes, for example, Ryle, Cook Wilson, Strawson, and Wittgenstein.[3] These philosophers have argued that the variables 'p', 'q', etc., as they appear in a schema such as that for *modus ponens* illustrated above, range over propositions or statements. They have maintained,

---

[2] P. T. Geach, 'Assertion', p. 452.

[3] G. Ryle, ' "If", "So" and "Because" ', in *Philosophical Analysis*, ed. M. Black, Cornell, 1950; J. Cook Wilson, *Statement and Inference*, Oxford, 1926; P. F. Strawson, *Introduction to Logical Theory*, London, 1952; L. Wittgenstein, *Tractatus Logico-Philosophicus*, London, 1922.

further, that it is a necessary condition for something's being a proposition or statement that it propose, state, or *assert* that something is the case. But if this were the case, then *modus tollens* would be a logical contradiction; for it contains within it an occurrence of '*p*' and an occurrence of 'not-*p*':

If *q* then *p*

But not-*p*

therefore not-*q*.

Ryle takes the heroic course of denying, therefore, that '*p*' and '*q*' as they occur within 'If *q* then *p*' are in fact statements or propositions. And this entails denying that the traditional truth-functional account of such conditional statements is accurate. Ryle suggests that we either treat 'If-*p*' and 'then-*q*' as indissoluble wholes, or we treat 'If *p* then *q*' as a *licence* to perform certain logical operations, and not as a statement or proposition. But such heroism is surely misplaced. Frege's argument shows that the actual possession or non-possession of assertive force is without bearing on questions of propositional identity. And his notation makes it quite clear when a proposition possesses assertive force. The proposition 'If *p* then *q*' is written in the concept-script as

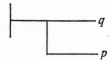

and this reveals that it is the complex as a whole to which assertive force attaches, and *not* to either '*p*' or '*q*' individually.

It is not, of course, solely on account of the existence of conditional statements that we must recognize that propositional identity is unaffected by assertive force; for they are in principle eliminable. In the disjunction 'either *p* or *q*' neither disjunct is asserted, and, more clearly still, '*p*' is not asserted in or by 'not-*p*'. Here there is another pitfall which Frege's perspicuous notation neatly avoids. For even though '*p*' is not asserted in or by 'not-*p*', this does not entail that 'not-*p*' does not make an assertion. Negation does not serve to *cancel* assertive force, but, as it were, to *reverse* it. In other words, the opposite of assertion is not denial, for a denial *is* an assertion:

'not-p' does not make no claim, it makes the claim that 'p' is false. Frege's sign for 'not-p' is

and the presence of the assertion stroke indicates, again, that the whole is asserted. The small vertical negation stroke which is attached to the content stroke indicates that 'negation is a mark of the content' of an assertion and in no way modifies the assertive force itself.

In the case of sub-sentential truth-functional contexts, then, Frege's use of the judgement stroke marks a valid and useful distinction, which enables us to avoid certain types of philosophical confusion. There is another type of context, however, in which a proposition may occur unassertively, and for which Frege failed to account. This is puzzling as there seems to be no reason why this should be so. Consider the following proof by *reductio* that $p \supset (q \supset p)$:

1.	$\sim (p \supset (q \supset p))$	Hypothesis.
2.	$p \,\&\sim (q \supset p)$	$\supset$ & Trans. (1)
3.	p	& Elim. (2)
4.	$\sim (q \supset p)$	& Elim. (2)
5.	$q \,\&\sim p$	$\supset$ & Trans. (4)
6.	$\sim p$	& Elim. (6)
7.	$p \,\&\sim p$	Conj. (3),(6)
8.	$\sim\sim (p \supset (q \supset p))$	Reductio, (1), (2–7)
9.	$p \supset (q \supset p)$	Double Neg. (Q.E.D.).

In this proof, premiss (1) is not something given as true; indeed it is known to be *false*. It is, rather, something *assumed* for the sake of the argument: a hypothesis or supposition. It cannot, therefore, be the case that premiss (1) as a whole possesses assertive force; and the conventions governing the layout of indirect proofs are designed precisely to indicate this fact. What falls outside the vertical bracket is to possess assertive force, as normal; but propositions which fall within this bracket occur non-assertively.

Now this case differs somewhat from the sub-sentential case

3. A LOGICAL DISTINCTION

examined earlier. For here it is not a propositional component that is devoid of assertive force, even though the whole proposition within which it occurs possesses this. Rather, it is a free-standing proposition as a whole, a *premiss* in an argument, which is without assertive force. This cannot be construed as a special case of the fomer type, by construing an argument as a proposition comprising the conjunction of its different steps; for this way lies the vicious infinite regress of Carroll's 'What the Tortoise said to Achilles'.[4]

It is difficult to know what Frege's attitude to indirect proofs was. Certainly he did not allow them to be formulated within the concept-script, as every step in a valid proof must be preceded by the assertion sign. (This is so because, for Frege, expressions preceded only by the horizontal stroke are mere *names*; and nothing can be validly and formally inferred from names.) Now if Frege had been unaware of the possibility of indirect proofs, then his omission would at least have been comprehensible. And if, on the other hand, Frege had denied that indirect proofs were possible, this would have been, simply, a mistake. But the situation is more puzzling than that. On the one hand he clearly acknowledged the possibility of valid indirect proofs: 'In an indirect proof', he wrote in *Verneinung*, 'knowledge of the truth is attained precisely through our grasping a false thought.' (*Vern*.145.) And in the *Begriffsschrift* too, he had written of indirect proofs as though they were entirely unobjectionable (see *Bs*.4). And yet Frege wrote in the comments he sent to Jourdain, on the latter's article 'The Development of the Theories of Mathematical Logic . . .':

A mere thought which is not recognized as true cannot be a premiss. Only after a thought has been recognized by me [*sic*] as true can it be a premiss for me. Mere hypotheses cannot be used as a premiss.[5]

This is a peculiar remark. Even more peculiar is Frege's statement in a private letter to Jourdain some two years later:

If a sentence which expresses a false thought is uttered with assertive force, it is logically useless and, precisely speaking, *unintelligible*.[6]

As against this one can only insist with Wittgenstein that 'One can draw inferences from a false proposition' (*TLP*.4.023). Conditional

---

[4] Lewis Carroll, 'What the Tortoise said to Achilles', *Mind*, iv (1895), 278–80.

[5] P. E. B. Jourdain, 'The Development of the Theories of Mathematical Logic and the Principles of Mathematics: Gottlob Frege', *QJPAM* xliii (1912), 237–69.

[6] Letter from Frege to Jourdain, undated but probably written in January 1914; *Brief*. 127.

proofs and other forms of indirect proof depend upon the very possibility which Frege is here denying, namely the possibility of discharging a hypothesis. Although I do not believe that Frege's attitude towards indirect proof can be made entirely comprehensible, a further attempt is made below, in section 5 of this chapter.

All this does not in any way, however, weaken his claim that propositional identity survives changes in assertiveness. Indeed, it is precisely this theory which must be understood if indirect proofs are to be intelligible. For to discharge a hypothesis is, precisely, to take a proposition (or its negation) from a context in which it is not asserted, and place it in a context in which it is.

4. A SYNTACTIC DISTINCTION

I wish now to take up the discussion of Frege's doctrine of assertion and his use of the two signs '|———' and '———' during the period 1891–1917, from the point at which we left it at the end of section 3, Chapter I. To summarize briefly: the introduction of the distinction between sense and reference (not formulated in the *Begriffsschrift*) and its application to sentences led to the claim that sentences are a species of complex complete name, which refer to their truth-values. But even granted that an indicative sentence refers to its truth-value, it is clear, and was clear to Frege, that it may also do more than this: it may assert that something is the case. In order to distinguish those cases in which a sentence merely refers to a truth-value from those cases in which it asserts something (and we have seen in the preceding section that there is need for some such distinction) Frege introduces, or reintroduces, the two signs '———' and '|———'. The explanation which he gives of them, however, is quite different from that offered in the *Begriffsschrift*. The sign

$$——— \xi$$

is a function-name denoting a function under which one and only one object falls: the True. We attempted to make sense of this doctrine by offering

ξ's being identical to the True

as a reading of this function-name. This reading has the merit of making clear that (i) assertive force is absent; (ii) a nominal role is intended; (iii) that only the True can fall under the concept thus denoted, and hence that the truth-conditions for '——— ξ' follow intuitively; and (iv), as Frege demands, that an expression which is the name of a truth-value always results when a referring proper name is substituted for 'ξ'. The possible arguments for this function do not, that is, have to be restricted to 'possible contents of judgement'. In the *Begriffsschrift* theory, that is,

——— Julius Caesar

would be malformed: Julius Caesar, being non-propositional, is not a 'possible content of judgement'. (Cf. *Bs*.2–4.) In the later theory, however, the function

——— ξ

was, like *all* functions, to be defined for any and every object (including Julius Caesar) as argument.

Now if I am right, the two signs '|———' and '———' can be employed to mark a syntactical distinction. On this reading the difference between

(1) |——— Δ

and

(2)   ——— Δ

where 'Δ' represents the content of the sentence 'This book is red', say, will represent the difference between the *sentence*

(3)   This book is red

and the *complex noun phrase*

(4)   This book's being red

or, equally:

> That this book is red
> The circumstance of this book's being red
> Red's being the colour of this book, etc.

Plainly the signs in question are not needed in ordinary language, where the possibility of such grammatical transformations exists. But in logic, or arithmetic, or in any field in which the possibility of such transformations is absent, this convention might well be adopted.

In the *Philosophical Investigations*, in a series of remarks addressed to the problem of assertion, Wittgenstein wrote:

Imagine a picture representing a boxer in a particular stance. Now this picture can be used to tell someone how he should stand, should hold himself, or how a certain man did stand in such and such a place; and so on. One might (using the language of chemistry) call this picture a *sentence radical*. This will be how Frege thought of the assumption (*Annahme*). (*PI*.12.)[7]

The Thought expressed by an indicative sentence (which Wittgenstein here mistakenly calls the *Annahme*) can also be expressed by the corresponding question, and by the corresponding nominalization. If this Thought is represented by a unary variable like '*p*' or '*Δ*', then (1) above will represent an indicative sentence, and (2) will represent the corresponding sentence radical. For the most appropriate form which we can give to a sentence radical is that of a complex noun phrase.

5. A PRAGMATIC DISTINCTION

The syntactical distinction between an indicative sentence and its nominalization, we have seen, is one which, in a perspicuous notation, the two signs '⊢——' and '——' might be employed to mark. We have also seen that Frege used them for this purpose. But not only for this purpose: the horizontal stroke and the judgement sign are also used, and at the same time, to mark a different distinction, and one that is rather more difficult to characterize. What we have to accomplish now is not just the elucidation of a Fregean doctrine, but the disentanglement of a piece of confusion.

In a footnote to *FuB*., Frege wrote:

The judgement sign [⊢——] cannot be used to construct a functional expression; for it does not serve, in conjunction with other signs, to designate an object. (*FuB*.22n.)

Now it follows from the account which Frege gives of the generation of function-names that predicates are function-names denoting functions which map objects on to truth-values. Predicates are

[7] (a) For the genesis and development of Russell's and Wittgenstein's confusions over the (Meinongian) notion of an *assumption* (*Annahme*), see G. E. M. Anscombe, *Introduction to Wittgenstein's Tractatus*, pp. 105–6. These confusions do not need to concern us here: we can read 'Thought' for 'assumption' in the passage quoted from the *Investigations*.
(b) Miss Anscombe translates *Satzradical* as 'proposition radical'. Although this may well be the best translation in the context in which it occurs, the use to which I wish to put the term makes 'sentence radical' a better translation.

obtained by the removal of one or more occurrences of a singular term from an indicative sentence. But if, as the above-quoted footnote asserts, the sign '⊢————' cannot be used to construct a function-name, and if any complex sign in which it occurs is not a denoting sign, it follows that any complex expression containing the judgement sign *cannot be a sentence*. For we know that, for Frege, sentences are names and can be used to construct function-names, viz. predicates.

If expressions beginning with the judgement stroke are not sentences, what are they? What contrast, over and above those noted in the immediately preceding sections, did Frege wish to draw by means of his use of the judgement and horizontal strokes? To answer these questions we must examine a train of thought which, despite his avowed intent to rid logic of its psychological appurtenances, Frege never managed to transcend. It is particularly obvious in passages like the following: 'No judgement is performed if the judgement stroke is absent. "———— A" merely requires the formulation of the *idea* that A is not the case.' (*Bs*.10.) 'According to the view I am here presenting, "5 > 4" and "1+3 = 5" just give us expressions for truth-values, without making any assertion. This separation of the act from the subject matter of judgement seems to me indispensable; for otherwise we could not express a mere supposition—the putting of a case without the simultaneous judgement as to its arising or not.' (*FuB*.21–2.) 'It must be pointed out once more, to grasp a Thought is not yet to judge.' (*Vern*.152.) In passages such as these, which span the whole of Frege's creative life, it is not assertive and unassertive occurrences of propositions that are being distinguished; nor yet sentences and sentence radicals. Rather, the distinction seems to concern human *acts* of different sorts (judging *vs.* supposing), or, perhaps, the distinction between an act and its content or object (my judging *vs.* what I judge).

The following, I believe, is as close an approximation as is possible to Frege's intention in using the judgement sign and the horizontal in the *Grundgesetze* and in *Funktion und Begriff*.[8]

The interpretation of the horizontal is unproblematic: it is a function-name which denotes a concept under which only the True falls, and for reasons already given is best read as a complex noun clause. Expressions which are preceded by the judgement stroke, on

[8] What follows is more a rational reconstruction than a straightforward statement of Frege's views. It is almost certain that Frege did not clearly distinguish the various elements he lumped together under the heading 'assertive force'.

the other hand, are to be regarded as *sentences-which-are-actually-asserted-to-be-true*. The action of placing the vertical assertion stroke before the horizontal effects two results: it transforms a noun clause into a sentence *and it asserts the Thought expressed by that sentence*. And so, in conformity with the original aims of the concept-script, Frege has taken what he believes to be a functionally ambiguous expression type (the sentence) and has replaced it with two expression types (⊢———— *Δ* and ———— *Δ*) which together perform all the roles of the sentence (or so Frege believes), but each one of which is unambiguous and univocal. A sentence can be used merely to present a hypothesis, to express a Thought; or it can be used to assert that a given Thought is true. The presenting of a hypothesis is performed by use of the *referring* sign '———— *Δ*', while the assertion that the hypothesis is true is performed by signs of the form '⊢———— *Δ*', and these latter, as Frege says, 'do not serve to denote anything; they assert something' (*FuB*.22n.).

If this interpretation is accepted, a number of otherwise perplexing characteristics of Frege's system become comprehensible. Take for example the matter of indirect proofs. We earlier found it difficult to understand why Frege outlawed such proofs from the *Begriffs-schrift*. But with the theory modified as it was after 1891, this becomes understandable (though not therewith acceptable): 'Only true Thoughts can be premisses of inferences. . . . It might be objected, however, that one can surely deduce conclusions from certain Thoughts purely hypothetically, without one's judging as to the truth of the latter. Precisely: purely hypothetically! But in this case the Thoughts in question are not the premisses of an inference. The premisses are, on the contrary, certain hypothetical Thoughts containing the Thoughts in question as their antecedents.'[9]

Put briefly the matter is thus: indirect proofs depend upon the possibility of an expression, or its negation, being used now as a hypothesis, and now as an assertion. But in construing this very possibility as a form of functional ambiguity, and in so rigorously pursuing the idea 'one job: one expression', Frege made such proofs impossible within the concept-script. In other words, nothing can be inferred, formally, from an expression of the form '———— *Δ*', because this is a *name* and does not *say* anything.[10] But on the other hand we

---

[9] 'Über die Grundlagen der Geometrie' (1906), p. 425. (Cf. also *Nach*.195 and *FPL*.309f.)

[10] One can, of course, infer things informally from a name. I can infer from the

cannot symbolize what is either known to be false, or what is not known to be true, by expressions of the form '⊢——— Δ', because such expressions *are* assertions, and so to do would be to lie! We can now, moreover, undertsand some of the strangely egocentric remarks which Frege makes about validity in proofs, e.g. 'Only when a thought has been recognized by me as true can it be a premiss for me'. That this should be the case follows from the fact that a premiss must be preceded by the judgement stroke, and this indicates that what follows it has been *asserted by someone*. The propositions preceded by the judgement stroke in the *Begriffsschrift*, for example, were asserted by Frege. 'We are probably best in accord with ordinary usage', Frege wrote, though in a slightly different connection, 'if we take judgement to be an act of judging, as a leap is an act of leaping. . . . If the judgement is an act, it happens at a certain time and thereafter belongs to the past. With an act there also belongs an agent, and we do not know the act completely if we do not know the agent.' (*Vern.*151n.) The expression '⊢———' stands, in use, as a record of an act of judgement performed by the person who wrote the sign.

Wittgenstein was thus right to say of the judgement stroke that 'in the works of Frege (and Russell) it simply indicates that these authors hold the proposition marked with this sign to be true' (*TLP*. 4.442). But Wittgenstein's further remarks in the same passage have given rise to a serious misconception which must be dealt with here. He writes: 'Frege's "judgement stroke" "⊢———" is logically quite meaningless' because 'it is quite impossible for a proposition to say of itself that it is true'. This is indeed impossible, and Frege's early *Begriffsschrift* account of assertion is open to an objection along these lines. His mature theory, however, is not. The sign '⊢———' does not say or state or assert that what follows it is held to be true; in Tractarian terms it *shows* this. The judgement sign cannot be translated into any explicit phrase or sentence. '⊢———' is not synonymous with 'it is asserted that', 'I assert', 'Gottlob Frege asserts that' . . . or indeed with any other such expression. This is because any such translation will materially alter the truth-conditions of any expression in which it occurs. Thus if we read '⊢——— 2+2 = 4' as 'It is asserted that 2+2 = 4', the latter but *not* the former

name 'Dr. B. Smith', for example, that its bearer is a doctor. It is clear, however, that 'Dr. B. Smith' does not *say* anything, does not make a claim that could be true or false. And for this reason it cannot constitute the premiss of an argument; and nor, for the same reason, can expressions of the form '——— Δ'.

will depend, not upon whether $2+2 = 4$, but upon whether this is asserted. In writing '⊢————' before a sentence one *is* asserting it, one is not claiming to assert it. The judgement stroke is, so to speak a *pure performative operator*.[11] Let us compare it with another performative operator, though not a pure one: 'I promise . . .'. It is generally acknowledged that someone who, under normal circumstances, utters the sentence 'I promise to come tomorrow' would therewith have performed an act of promising. And in uttering such a sentence one is not reporting or describing an act of promising, but, rather, promising. This is not the case, however, when the verb *to promise* is used in other tenses than the present and in other persons than the first person singular or plural. 'He promised to come' is not a promise, and neither is 'I promised to come'. 'I promise' is a performative verb, which can also be used in non-performative ways, e.g. to describe, report, and so on. In contrast, the judgement sign is used to bring off the act of assertion, but cannot be used to report or describe acts of assertion; otherwise it would contribute materially to the truth-conditions of expressions in which it occurred. (It would, for one thing, change a direct occurrence of '*p*' into an oblique one, thus, for Frege, changing the reference of '*p*' from its truth-value to its (normal) sense.) And even if we interpret the judgement sign as, say, 'I assert' and stipulate that it is to 'suffer change neither of tense nor of subject' (*FPL*.335), still this would be inadequate. For the judgement sign, if it is to perform the function for which it was intended, namely the distinguishing of assertive from unassertive occurrences of propositions, must be incapable of appearing within a subordinate clause. But, of course, 'I assert that *p*' can occur as a subordinate clause, say as the antecedent of a conditional statement: 'If I assert that *p*, then . . .'. And here neither 'I assert that *p*' nor '*p*' is asserted.

Such, then, is the result to which we are led by taking to its logical conclusion Frege's *Grundgesetze* account of the judgement stroke. The entities with which logic deals are neither sentences nor propositions, but bear a striking resemblance to what have lately come to be known as *interiorized speech acts*: mental acts whose linguistic counterpart is the assertive utterance of a declarative sentence. This mental act Frege calls 'judgement': 'When we acknowledge internally that something is true, we judge; and when we express the judgement,

[11] This account was formulated independently of, but is in many respects similar to that given by Dummett; see *FPL*.333–6.

we assert.' (*Nach*.2.) I shall not concern myself with the merits of this doctrine as far as concerns logic, but will examine some of the interesting extensions that can be made to it in the analysis of the notion of *judgement*.

6. JUDGING AND WONDERING

We can distinguish between assertive and unassertive mental acts in a way directly analogous to the way in which we distinguished between assertive and unassertive occurrences of propositions. We can distinguish, that is, between mental acts, or states of mind, which involve the agent or possessor in a commitment to the truth of some claim, and those which involve no such commitment. Consider, for example, the following two lists:

Group A	Group B
wondering	judging
thinking about	thinking that
pondering	believing
examining	acknowledging
considering	denying
imagining	agreeing
supposing . . . etc.	remembering that . . . etc.

Group *A* comprises those acts and attitudes which involve the possessor in no commitment to the truth of some claim that such and such is the case. Thus, when I wonder if it is raining I neither assert nor judge nor deny that it is, or is not, raining. One might say that, intentionally or unintentionally, I am keeping an open mind on the matter. The acts and attitudes which fall within Group *B*, on the other hand, do commit the agent or possessor to the truth of the corresponding claim; this is evident in that my judgement, my belief, etc. can be either correct or incorrect, true or false.

Both types of act may have what Frege called the same conceptual content. That which is the object of my wondering may also (though not at one and the same time) be the object of my act of judgement. After wondering if it is raining I may go to the window and ascertain that, in fact, it *is* raining. What I previously wondered about, and what I subsequently judge to be the case are one and the same; only my attitude has undergone a change. If this were not the case, then, for example, an experiment could not confirm a hypothesis; for what is confirmed as being the case would be different from what was previously embodied in the hypothesis. Frege's notation can, therefore, be used to mark this distinction: *wondering whether* Δ will be represented as

$$\text{------} \Delta$$

while *judging that* Δ will become

$$\vdash\!\text{------} \Delta.$$

Some such distinction, between types of internal act, seems to lie behind the *Begriffsschrift* use of the horizontal stroke and the judgement sign:

> If we omit the little vertical stroke . . . the judgement is to be transformed into a mere complex of ideas; the author is not expressing his recognition or non-recognition of the truth of this. (*Bs*.2.)

At this point it will be well to get clear about *expressions*. People are said to express not only judgements but feelings and thoughts, and sentences as well; and sentences are also said to express thoughts as well as truths. In the first place, then, we can distinguish between *internal* and *external acts of judgement*. An internal act of judgement is a mental act which (like deciding, day-dreaming, or wanting a cigarette) may on any given occasion on which it occurs not result in any overt physical behaviour whatsoever. An external act of judgement is an overt, physical act of some sort. External acts of judgement may be either linguistic or non-linguistic. I might express my judgement of a particular theatrical production, for instance, by saying 'That was appalling' (a linguistic act) or by throwing garden produce at the performers (a non-linguistic act). A linguistic external act of judgement may be either sentential or non-sentential.

I shall use the phrase an *S-expression of a judgement* in this sense: 'it is raining', 'es regnet', and 'il pleut' are all S-expressions for the judgement that it is raining. And so an S-expression, as I shall use the phrase, must always be a meaningful sentence in the indicative mood. An *A-expression of a judgement*, on the other hand, is an action, and as such must be a datable performance by an agent. Plainly no S-expression can be an A-expression: no sentence can be an action. Yet, equally plainly, there is the closest relation between these categories; for it is by uttering a sentence that one paradigmatically expresses a judgement. To utter the sentence 'it is raining' is to A-express the judgement which is S-expressed by 'es regnet'. Though here we have an ambiguity in the term 'judgement' as well. This can be resolved, provisionally, by stipulating that the terms related by the two expressive relations are as follows: a sentence-type S-expresses a proposition; a person (or an act) A-expresses a judgement. The relation *A-expresses*, then, relates internal and external acts of judgement. The diagram (Fig. 6) makes clear the distinctions and terminology I have introduced; though it must be emphasized here that these do not, and are not meant to, constitute even the beginnings of a theory of judgement. This marks merely the establishment of a provisional terminology based on distinctions which have been taken over from both common sense and the history of philosophy, but into whose import and appropriateness we have yet to inquire.

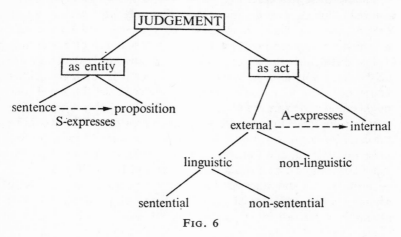

FIG. 6

7. THE MODALITY OF JUDGEMENT *VS*. THE JUDGEMENT OF MODALITY

In the preceding section we distinguished briefly those psychological attitudes and acts which do, from those which do not, involve a commitment, on the part of the person who has or does them, to the truth or falsity of a claim that something is the case. We took as paradigmatic of the former sort *judging*, and of the latter sort *wondering*. In section 5 we saw that the sign '⊢————' could be used as a pure performative operator, used in performing the act of assertion. We must now ask whether these two uses are compatible, and whether there is need for a corresponding performative operator for the act of wondering.

Let us examine the following sentences:

(1) It is raining.

(2) I wonder whether it is raining.

(3) Perhaps it is raining.

(4) It is possible that it is raining.

To utter sentence (1) would constitute an adequate A-expression of a judgement,[12] while sentence (2) might well be employed to express a wondering. Given that the object of the judgement expressed by (1) is the same as that of the wondering expressed by (2), we might symbolize these two cases as '⊢——— Δ' and '——— Δ' respectively. But the following considerations show that only *internal* acts may be thus represented. There seems to be an asymmetry between the ways in which we may represent internal and external acts of wondering.

The distinguishing feature of acts of wondering is that they are neither true nor false. In wondering whether it is raining I neither affirm nor deny that it is raining. Yet the sentence (2), which one might employ to express a wondering, is clearly capable of possessing a truth-value, and could be uttered with assertive force. This would be the case, for instance, if I were asked what I do when I hear a tapping noise on the roof, and I answer 'I wonder whether it is raining'. My reply asserts that I perform a certain act, and is true if in fact I do perform this act and otherwise false. It appears, then, that there is an asymmetry between internal and external acts of wondering which is absent from the activity of judging, For an interior act of wondering is, *ex hypothesi*, without assertive force, and can be represented by the horizontal stroke; whereas the sign '⊢———' can be used to represent either an interior or an exterior act of judging (both are assertive) *or* an exterior act of wondering. Now this asymmetry might well be taken as indicating that there is some private or ineffable aspect to wondering which is absent from judging. In my opinion much that is unacceptable in Frege's account of judgement stems from some such misconstrual. Notice, for instance, how he omits from the following list any external linguistic act corresponding to the interior act of wondering. 'We may distinguish', he writes (*Ged*.62):

---

[12] Henceforth I shall not usually indicate whether it is an A-expression or an S-expression that is in question, as this will usually be clear from the context.

(i)   the apprehension of a thought [interior act of wondering].
(ii) the recognition of the truth of a thought [interior act of judging].
(iii) the manifestation of this judgement [exterior act of judging].

Time and again Frege's attitude seems to be that, while judging and asserting are activities which may occur in the objective, intersubjective world, such activities as wondering or grasping a thought are ineluctably interior: private to the person who performs them. And so, while a judgement can be a *truth*, a wondering can be only a 'mere complex of *ideas*' (cf. *Bs*.2–4). But we cannot allow that there are public judgements with private contents; some way must be found of representing wonderings without giving them assertive force, on the one hand, or relagating them to some shadowy realm of the purely subjective, on the other.

It will be helpful if we first examine sentences (3) and (4), as the issues are somewhat more clearly defined here. In the language of common discourse both sentences can be used to make an assertion (about a possibility) or to express a wondering (about the weather). Possibilities, just as well as actualities and necessities, may constitute the subject-matter of assertions. But one can also hedge one's bets and refuse to commit oneself to the truth or falsity of a given proposition, by saying 'Perhaps that's the case (and perhaps it isn't)'. Frege makes just this point when he writes:

If a proposition is presented as possible, then either the speaker is refraining from judgement . . . or else he is saying that in general the negation of the proposition is false. In the latter case we have what is usually termed a particular affirmative judgement. (*Bs*.5.)

'It is possible that Δ' (or more colloquially: 'perhaps Δ') can be symbolized as either

(5) $\models\!\!\!-\!\!\!-\ (\lozenge\ \Delta)$[13]

or

(6) $-\!\!\!-\!\!\!-\ \Delta.$

(5) is a judgement of possibility; (6) is a possible judgement.

Now if this is right, then there is no longer any reason to deny that Frege's threefold division can be extended so as to cover all four parts of the two intersecting distinctions between internal/external and assertive/non-assertive acts as follows:

[13] '$\lozenge$' is the modal operator for *possibility*.

(i)   Wondering (internal non-assertive act)
(ii)   Judging (internal assertive act)
(iii)   Expressing a wondering (non-assertive locutionary act)
(iv)   Expressing a judgement (assertive locutionary act).

This fourfold division is again examined, below, in Chapter IV.

8. SUMMARY

At this point we have mentioned seven prima facie distinct uses to which the concept-script signs '⊢———' and '———' might have been put by Frege; and, with one exception, we have seen that there is indeed a valid distinction that can be marked in these cases. But what are we to say of Frege's philosophical motivation, over and above noting that it was somewhat confused? Can a univocal reading be given to the so-called judgement sign and the horizontal stroke? I think the answer is no. But we can make considerable progress in the direction of reducing the chaos which Frege bequeathed.

In the first place, there are *two* fundamental notions of assertion or assertive force. One notion, the more basic for Frege, is the 'logical' notion examined in section 3 above. The test for deciding whether a given proposition occurs assertively within a given context is the test of exportation: if the proposition can be removed from that context without further ado, and displayed on a line in a proof by itself, then that proposition is asserted in the original context. Thus 'p' occurs assertively in 'p & q' but not in either 'if p then q' or 'not-p'. As a limiting case, of course, 'p' occurs assertively in 'p', and 'if p then q' occurs assertively in 'if p then q'. Which is to say that any free-standing, unembedded proposition possesses assertive force, as far as concerns the needs of logic. But this test explains nothing: it is exportation that is explained and justified by the possession by a proposition of assertive force, and not the reverse. Still, this logical notion of assertion is one which Frege is right to indicate in his concept-script; for it is an objective phenomenon which must be recognized if validity is not to be vitiated, and which should, therefore, be embodied in a perspicuous notation. This is not to deny that the possession or absence of assertive force is usually so obvious intuitively that it can remain unmarked without danger; but a perspicuous notation sets itself the aim of making explicit such hidden but effective forces, no matter how obvious they may be.

The second, different, though closely analogous notion of assertion attaches to speech acts and to their interior, mental counterparts. Here assertion is a human action; it is something which a certain person does with a certain proposition at a certain time. This is done when a person commits himself to the truth of that proposition, and this he may do either out loud, or to himself. The paradigmatic form of an exterior assertion is the uttering of an indicative sentence. As Frege rightly insisted the 'assertion sign' of ordinary language, so to speak, lies in the indicative mood of the verb. Yet there are contexts of utterance (and tones of voice etc.) which will rob an utterance of assertive force. For instance, I may say firmly and with conviction 'Someone has just stolen your car', but if I am taking part in an elocution class or a theatrical performance I will not be taken to have asserted anything.

The judgement and horizontal strokes are, then, systematically ambiguous syncategoremata: they have no independent meaning outside contexts of certain types, and there are basically *two* such context types. If—merely as an exegetical device—we adopt the convention of distinguishing these contexts by employing propositional constants of differing typographical style, then we can make the ambiguity clear as follows: The sign '⊢———' can be used in logic to mark the presence of assertive force. Thus *modus ponens* can be written:

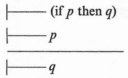

And this shows that only one occurrence of 'p' is assertive. The horizontal stroke, without the vertical assertion stroke, will represent the nominalization of the corresponding sentence. This corresponds closely with Frege's intentions in the *Grundgesetze*, as established in section 4 above. If, on the other hand, a different typography is used (the capital Greek letters 'Δ' and 'Γ' say) then a different reading is to be given: '⊢——— Δ' will represent *the judgement that Δ*, while '——— Δ' will represent *the content of this act*.

Now, so far, this accords well with the intentions which Frege embodied in his mature works. So well, in fact, that we can now accomplish something which Frege also wished to accomplish, but was unable. We wish to use the signs '⊢———' and '———' to distinguish between certain kinds of mental act: judging and wondering.

But if these signs are employed to mark the distinction between *an act* of judgement and its *content* or object, they cannot simultaneously be used to distinguish between types of acts. For otherwise '——— $\varDelta$' would have to represent both the content of the judgement that $\varDelta$, and the act of wondering whether $\varDelta$. And this is a nonsensical assimilation. As was pointed out above (section 7), it is at just this point that Frege's doctrine is left incomplete so as to avoid explicit contradiction. But we can, following a hint of Frege's, introduce a new sign to represent the act of wondering. We perform an act of wondering, Frege says, 'when we formulate a propositional question' (*Ged.*62). And so if '⊢——— $\varDelta$' represents the judgement that $\varDelta$, '?——— $\varDelta$' will represent the act of wondering whether $\varDelta$. Both acts have the same content: ——— $\varDelta$.

We have, then, introduced a systematic ambiguity into the judgement sign and the horizontal stroke, albeit one which is easily resolved in use; and we have introduced, what Frege never did, a special sign for the act of wondering, or formulating a hypothesis. We have, however, preserved Frege's important insights that there are the closest analogies between the logical and the pragmatic aspects of assertion, between sentences and their nominalizations and propositional attitudes and the propositions which are their objects.

We must now discover in greater detail what it is that signs like '$\varDelta$' mean, what a Fregean Thought or proposition is.

CHAPTER IV

THE THOUGHT

Ich gebrauche das Wort 'Gedanke' ungewöhnlich.—Frege.

1. INTRODUCTION

AT this point we have already provided an account of the notion of *sense* as it applies to proper names (Chapter II, Section 4) and a preliminary account of how it applies to predicates (Chapter II, section 6). It remains to be shown how these two theories come together to provide an account of sentence sense, and how this notion (or, as it will transpire, these notions) relate to the act of judgement.

The title of the present chapter is ambiguous: our subject-matter will comprise not only an examination of 'the Thought', Frege's term for the sense of a declarative sentence, but also of 'The Thought' ('Der Gedanke'), Frege's essay of 1918 in which he propounded his final theory of judgement.[1] This final theory differs somewhat from that offered in the earlier works, and we must spend some time establishing in what ways the theory changed, and whether these changes are acceptable.

The following section comprises a brief examination of some of the less desirable elements in Frege's later theory; specifically, his naïve platonic realism, faculty psychology, and associationist theory of meaning-intention. I shall not attempt to provide a detailed refutation of these doctrines, but will merely show that each is a *ramus amputandus*: what is essential and valuable in Frege's theory will stand without them.

2. 'DER GEDANKE'

As with so much of Frege's work, the essay of 1918 (along with the other parts of the *Logische Untersuchungen*) was motivated in large

---

[1] Though the present chapter concentrates upon Frege's 1918 essay 'Der Gedanke', these remarks must not be taken to imply that the other parts of the *Logische Untersuchungen* are exceptions to these generalizations about Frege's philosophical position after 1918.

part by the desire to combat the then widespread importation of psychological and merely subjective elements into logic and the foundations of mathematics. Frege's aim was to 'prevent the blurring of the boundaries between psychology and logic' (*Ged*.59). And in this respect 'Der Gedanke' takes its place along side the other major works in the mainstream of Fregean thought. In most other respects, however, it is exceptional.

Perhaps the first unusual thing to strike the reader familiar only with the earlier works is the style and tone in which it is written. One notices, for example, the complete absence of any special symbolism or formalization; the appeal to examples drawn from history, literature, and ordinary life, rather than from arithmetic and the formal sciences; and, in general, the shift from the esoteric to the quotidian. If the historical origins of the formal approach to language and philosophy (as exemplified subsequently in the works of Carnap, Tarski, Quine, and Church, say,) can be located in the *Begriffsschrift* and the *Grundgesetze*, then surely 'Der Gedanke' constitutes one of the earliest examples of what has come to be known as the philosophy of ordinary language. The changed style and emphasis embodied in Frege's late works can, I believe, be traced to two sources. One is the disenchantment he no doubt felt with the purely formal approach to logic and language after the discovery by Russell in 1902 of the paradox to which his system gives rise.[2] We can also speculate that the visits paid by the young Wittgenstein after about 1911 were influential in this respect. The difference which resulted can best be characterized by saying that in 'Der Gedanke' Frege is primarily interested in the possibility of human communication (albeit the communication of factual information) and not, as previously, in the construction of a perspicuous notation for the deduction and expression of 'truths of reason'.

What chiefly concerns us here are the philosophical doctrines concerning Thought, judgement, sense, etc. which Frege propounded after 1918, and the difference between these and those of the earlier works. Two such differences have already been noted: (i) in addition to indicative sentences, certain kinds of interrogative sentence are now admitted to be capable of expressing a Thought. These are the so-called 'propositional questions' (*Satzfragen*), that is, ones which can be answered 'yes' or 'no'. (ii) *No* appeal is now made to the once central doctrines that a sentence refers to its truth-value, that

[2] See Appendix, below.

function-names refer to functions, or that predicates refer to concepts. The emphasis is now shifted completely from the 'realm of reference' to the 'realm of sense'.

Even a cursory reading of 'Der Gedanke' reveals that Frege is there relying upon a definite and very traditional theory of human nature, its powers and faculties. The theory runs, with depressing familiarity, as follows: Man's mental powers are to be divided into those cognitive and those volitional. The cognitive faculties include perception and reason; the will is the volitional faculty which translates the activities of the cognitive faculties into action. 'How does a Thought act?' Frege asks. 'By being apprehended and taken to be true. This is a process in the inner world of a thinker . . . which, encroaching on the sphere of the will, can make itself noticeable in the outer world.' (*Ged*.76.) Thoughts, Frege agrees with Plato, are eternal, immutable essences which are neither created, nor sustained, nor in any way altered by any human activity; nor are they perceivable by any human sense. And so, Frege concludes, they exist neither in the external material world, nor in the subjective inner world: 'a third realm must be recognized' (*Ged*.69). But having posited this 'third realm' whose denizens are Thoughts, Frege must allow the possibility of human contact with it—otherwise thinking would be impossible. He is led, therefore, to posit the existence of a special faculty whose function is the contemplation of eternal truths and falsehoods. (Cf. *Ged*.74.)

Now such doctrines as these represent the tip of an ugly ontological iceberg. The later essays of Frege are hallmarked by an overwillingness to indulge in the hypostatization of 'realms', 'spheres', and 'worlds'. Apart from the realm of reference and the realm of sense, there is the inner world and the outer world, the realms of the actual and the non-actual, and of the subjective and the objective. Some idea of the complexity of the resulting architectonic can be gained by observing that while all these distinctions to some extent overlap, no two are coincident. Thoughts, for example, are actual, objective, belong to the realm of sense, but are apprehended in the inner world by a special faculty. A sensation is actual, subjective, and belongs to the realm of reference and the inner world. A number, on the other hand, is non-actual, objective, and belongs to the realm of reference. Much of this ontologizing is, indeed, harmless and can be easily translated into more acceptable terms. The tendency has one unacceptable result, however, which concerns the relations between the realms of reference and sense. For Frege these two realms are disjoint; at least this is the doctrine of 'Der Gedanke'. (Cf. also *SuB*.35.) But this cannot be the case, for the simple reason that one can refer to a sense. In the sentence 'Mark Anthony said that Brutus was an honourable man', for instance, the expression 'Brutus was an honourable man' *refers* to a Thought, a sense. Moreover, given Frege's way of distinguishing functions and objects, a Thought, being complete, is an object. Thiel has accurately characterized this confusion on Frege's part as 'the contamination of semantic role with ontological status'. The distinction between sense and reference is a semantic distinction; it cannot be used to mark out two ontological realms; for senses can be referred to.[3]

Because, for Frege, Thoughts exist prior to and independently of their being grasped or expressed by any person, he is forced to represent the relations between a person and a Thought, and also between a Thought and the language which expresses it, as arbitrary and non-complex. He writes at times as though a person were possessed of a stock of sentences which he could, as the need arose, associate with Thoughts he had apprehended and which he wished to express. By uttering such a sentence he then tries to bring it about that the same Thought is apprehended by another person: 'One communicates a Thought. How does this happen? One brings about changes in the common outside world which, perceived by another person, are *supposed* to *induce* him to apprehend *a* thought.' (*Ged*.77, my italics.) The difficulties inherent in this model are brought to the fore by the italicized phrases in this last quoted sentence. When a speaker utters a sentence with the intention of communicating a Thought, his words are not 'supposed to induce' the hearer to apprehend some Thought. In the first place, causally to induce a Thought to enter another person's mind is not an activity we would normally call a form of *communication*. If, for example, I possessed a drug which, when administered, brought it about that the recipient thought that snow is white, it would be wrong to say that in administering this drug I was communicating the Thought that snow is white. But on the other hand, when I *say* that snow is white I am not performing an act with which I hope my hearer will associate a Thought (preferably, of course, the Thought that snow is white). On the contrary, I know that if my hearer understands English he will

---

[3] C. Thiel, *Sense and Reference in Frege's Logic*, pp. 89–92.

understand my words, and *in so doing* he will understand the Thought
I wish to communicate. The notion of an act of association performs
no useful function here, and this is reason enough to dispense with it.
This naïve associationist model has, however, further more serious
consequences for Frege's theory of judgement. For, as Wittgenstein
has taught us to expect, it leads to a radical linguistic scepticism. 'Yet
there is a doubt', confesses Frege, 'is it at all the *same* Thought
which first one person expresses and now another?' (*Ged*.65.) There
is no possibility of answering this question by appeal to the associationist model; for we never have access to the apprehension of
Thoughts by another, but only to the signs he uses. We can never,
therefore, know whether the Thought he has apprehended is the same
as the Thought which we have associated with a given sentence. Or,
rather, which *I* have associated with a given sentence: we have lost
all right to appeal to a common, intersubjective language. This
analysis of the communication situation results, not in a mild form of
problematical scepticism about the possibility of successful communication, but rather in a fundamental incoherence: linguistic
solipsism. If the notion of a Thought with which a person associates
a given sentence is to fulfil the function required of it in a theory of
judgement and communication, then it must be possible for the
Thought to be identified *independently* of the language with which it
is associated. Now clearly this is not possible for a given person when
the act of association is not his own; a fact which Frege recognized
and accepted; a fact which makes a problematical scepticism with
respect to the possibility of successful communication inescapable.
What Frege did not realize, and what Wittgenstein has shown, is that
a person cannot identify a Thought independently of the language in
which it may be expressed, *even in his own case*: 'If you say: "How
can I know what he means when I see only the signs he gives?" then
I say: "how is *he* to know what he means, when he has nothing but
the signs either?"' (*PG*.40.) The associationist model depends upon
the speaker (and the hearer) making the *right* association between
Thought and sentence; yet this model is incapable of providing an
explanation of how this is possible. 'One wants to say: whatever is
going to seem right to me is right. And this only means that here we
can't talk about "right".' (*PI*.92.) In the absence of any means of
distinguishing between right and wrong uses of an expression, however, there can be no means of distinguishing between meaningful and
meaningless uses of language. In other words, the concept *meagnin*

can find no application here—a disastrous result for a theory of meaning and communication.

My primary concern is not the refutation of what is objectionable in Frege's theory, but rather the justification and expansion of what is defensible and illuminating. Accordingly I shall henceforth ignore his crude associationism and the faculty psychology with which it is buttressed, and pass on to more interesting matters.

3. INPUT SENSE AND OUTPUT SENSE

We can begin by examining the two Fregean principles for the determination of complex reference and sense:

$PS1$: The sense of a sentence is determined by the senses of its component parts,

and

$PR2$: The truth-value of a sentence is determined by its sense. (And, of course, how things stand.)

These two principles depend for their plausibility and usefulness upon there being a sense of 'sense' which remains constant throughout.

Now the first principle, $PS1$, might be thought false on the following grounds. The sense of a sentence is not exhaustively determined by the senses of the component expressions because, in many cases, the context of utterance is also a crucially important factor. This would seem to be the case most clearly when the sentence in question contains token reflexive or indexical elements. Thus the sense expressed by the sentence 'I ate plum-pudding today', in so far as this sense is capable of determining a truth-value via $PR2$, must itself be determined in part by contextual factors: who says it, and when. Frege allows that this is, indeed, the case, but insists that this is an inessential and undesirable property of the language of common discourse. Any information which, either from laziness or convenience, we allow to remain tacitly contained in the context of utterance *could*, he maintains, be explicitly stated in the sentence. (It is just this claim that I shall contest in the sequel.) The more nearly a language approaches the ideals of clarity, objectivity, precision, and universality, Frege argues, the less will the truth-conditions of its sentences depend upon accidents of their utterances. Contextually dependent items must, therefore, be expanded and rendered explicit so that their contextual dependence is severed. Then it will be the sentence *per se* which expresses a sense capable of being either true or false. And so, rather than say 'I ate plum-pudding today', one ought to say something of the form: 'I, so and so, ate plum-pudding today, the such and such'. In this way one will have *said* something which is either true or false, and not merely implied or suggested it. We will return to this matter in a moment.

A second objection to *PS1* might run as follows: it is not merely the senses of the component expressions which determine the sense of a sentence, because the *order* in which the expressions occur is also relevant. 'Caesar loved Cleopatra' and 'Cleopatra loved Caesar' are two sentences, the objection runs, with the same components, but which clearly express different senses. And this difference in sense seems to be a function of the different word orders. We have already argued against this position (Chapter II, section 6); and here it is sufficient to observe that this objection depends upon our construing the elements of a sentence as being the words which compose it. But Frege's categorial grammar does not analyse these two sentences into the constituents 'Caesar', 'Cleopatra', and 'loved'; but rather into the two proper names 'Caesar' and 'Cleopatra' and the two-placed predicate '( ) loved ( )'. But then, if the sense of an expression is what one understands when one is able to use that expression correctly, the order of insertion of singular terms into the argument-places of this predicate is clearly a part of the sense of that predicate. In other words, if someone did not know that insertion in the order: '*a* loved *b*' expresses a different sense from that in the order: '*b* loved *a*', then we could not say of that person that he understood the predicate '( ) loved ( )'.

The principle *PS1*, I shall argue, demands a notion of *sense* which is, *pace* Frege, different from that demanded by *PR2*. In other words, just as we earlier discovered that implicit in Frege's semantical theory were two notions of reference, so we can also discover two distinct notions of sense. We can discover in the Fregean notion of sense two conflicting elements which, following a suggestion of Wiggins, I shall call the 'input sense' and the 'output sense' of an expression.[4]

We can begin at an intuitive level by observing the peculiarity of Frege's claim that it is the sense or meaning of a sentence which is

[4] D. Wiggins, 'On Sentence Sense, Word Sense and Difference of Word Sense. . . . ', in *Semantics. An Interdisciplinary Reader*, ed. D. D. Steinberg and L. A. Jacobovits, p. 24.

primarily either true or false: 'When we say a sentence is true', he writes, 'we really mean its sense is' (*Ged.*60). To this one wants to respond that what a sentence *says*, or is used to say, may well be true; but its *meaning* cannot be either true or false. Equally peculiar, and for much the same reasons, is the claim that the objects of thought are meanings or senses. To say that I believe that I shall have plum-pudding tomorrow does not, prima facie, seem to mean the same as saying that I believe the *meaning* of the sentence 'I shall have plum-pudding tomorrow'. It is difficult to conceive what it might be to 'believe a meaning' or 'believe a sense'. My intuition is that there is here some categorial transgression analogous to that involved in talk of 'asserting an object', 'hearing a number', or 'kicking an emotion' (when these phrases are intended non-metaphorically). We must see whether this intuition can be substantiated.

Let us examine the two sentences:

(1) I ate plum-pudding today

and

(2) Today I ate plum-pudding.

Although these sentences belong to two different types, they can be admitted to express *the same meaning*, in some sense of that term. It seems clear, too, that this meaning is determined by the senses of the component elements, in conformity with *PS1*. It will be this meaning, moreover, which is preserved by any correct translation of these sentences into another language. I shall call the concept thus partially isolated the input sense or, simply, the meaning, of an expression. Synonymy, then, is the relation of identity for input senses or meanings. Expressions which express an input sense are not necessarily sentential; for otherwise (i) *PS1* would lose all plausibility, and (ii) we should not be able to say of two words or phrases that they are synonymous.

Now while the input sense of (1) is the same as that of (2), it is different from that of

(3) Yesterday you ate plum-pudding.

This is so because 'today' does not mean the same as 'yesterday', 'I' does not mean the same as 'you'. But if a person *A* said sentence (1) (or (2)) on a given Monday, and on the following Tuesday another person *B* said sentence (3) to *A*, then there would be a sense in which they had both *said the same thing*, viz. that *A* ate plum-pudding that

Monday. We have a choice of locutions here: we can say that *A* and *B* both express the same proposition, that they make the same statement or claim, that they assert the same thing, or express the same thought. But choice of any of the terms 'statement', 'thought', 'proposition', etc. will no doubt seem in this context to be the tacit invocation of some philosophical theory. Fewer questions will be begged, and will seem to have been begged, if we coin a special term for what it is that *A*'s utterance of (1) and *B*'s utterance of (3) have in common. I shall call this the *output sense* of the expressions. Unlike input sense, output sense is essentially sentential.

The need for some such distinction as this has been argued on a number of occasions by contemporary philosophers.[5] But, to the best of my knowledge, all have maintained that the essential difference between what I have called a sentence's meaning and its output sense is that while the truth-value of the former may change, the truth-value of the latter is fixed and invariant for all time. Frege subscribes to this doctrine (cf. *Ged.*64–5). The clearest statement of this view, however, is provided by E. J. Lemmon: 'Sentences will vary their truth-values . . . from context to context; so for that matter will propositions, as the [input] senses of sentences. By contrast, statements [i.e. output senses] are true or false once and for all. The statement that Brutus killed Caesar is true for all time.'[6] Lemmon's argument for the need to distinguish between sentences, their input senses, and their output senses (he calls the last two 'propositions' and 'statements' respectively) is grounded in the need to resolve the 'deep seated ambiguity in the notion of *saying the same thing*'. Two people can 'say the same thing' either by uttering the same sentence, by uttering different sentences which have the same meaning, or by uttering sentences so as to make the same claim: 'If I say "I am hot" and you, being French, say "J'ai chaud", then we have neither uttered the same sentence, nor made the same statement; but there is still a sense in which we have said the same thing, namely expressed the same sense.' With this I am in complete accord; but nothing here commits one to the position that input senses may be true or false.

---

[5] See, e.g., J. Teichman, 'Propositions', *Phil. Rev.* lxx (1961), 500–17; R. Cartwright, 'Propositions', in *Analytical Philosophy*, ed. R. J. Butler (1st series), Oxford, 1962, pp. 81–103; E. J. Lemmon, 'Sentences, Statements and Propositions', in *British Analytical Philosophy*, ed. B. Williams and A. Montefiore, London, 1966, pp. 87–107.

[6] E. J. Lemmon, op. cit., p. 97.

The crucial difference between meanings and output senses is not that the truth-values of the former may change while those of the latter are invariant, but that the former do not possess truth-values at all. The *substantial* issues concerning reference (by which I mean whether or not an expression actually succeeds in referring, and if so, to what) do not concern the notion of an expression's input sense. (This was discussed in more detail above, Chapter II, section 5.) Such sentences as 'The present King of France is bald', 'Odysseus was set ashore at Ithaca while sound asleep', and the like, express a sense irrespective of whether or not the singular terms occurring within them actually refer. This, of course, is a central Fregean doctrine: 'If it were only a question of the sense of the sentence, the Thought, it would be unnecessary to bother with the reference of a part of the sentence; only the sense, not the reference, of the part is relevant to the sense of the whole.' (*SuB*.33.) Now this doctrine *can* only apply to the input sense of an expression; for as we have seen, sub-sentential expressions do not have output sense. On the other hand, however, the substantial issues concerning reference *do* affect the output sense, if any, of a sentence. If a singular term which does not refer, in fact, to anything occurs as the subject term of a declarative sentence, then that sentence will not express an output sense. For in (putatively) asserting of the present king of France that he is bald, I am not in fact asserting baldness of anything: there *is* no present king of France. There is here only pseudo-assertion just as, and just because, there is here only pseudo-reference.

If the substantial issues concerning reference do not affect the input sense or meaning of a sentence, the *formal* or grammatical issues concerning reference do. The input sense of the sentence 'Odysseus was set ashore at Ithaca while sound asleep', for example, is in part determined by the input sense of the proper name 'Odysseus'. And as we have already seen, it is part of the latter that the name purports to refer to a man called Odysseus.

These considerations lend weight to the claim that (i) input sense and output sense are to be distinguished, and (ii) input senses are never true or false. For if what is primarily true or false is the assertion, *of* some object, *that* it possesses a given characteristic, then the possession of reference by the subject term of the sentence employed to make this claim will be a necessary condition of its being either true or false. Sentential input sense, on the other hand, is insensitive to success or failure of reference. One can significantly assert that the input sense of the two sentences 'I am hot' and 'J'ai chaud' is the same; but one cannot ask whether it is true. As a matter of fact, both Frege and Lemmon would agree that such a sentence as 'I am hot' does not express a meaning which is either true or false. But they would assert this on the grounds that the meaning of this sentence is too *indeterminate* to possess a truth-value, not that meanings are not the sort of thing that can be said to be true or false. And here we must take up the discussion of the relevance of the context of utterance, mentioned at the beginning of this section. Lemmon repeats the Fregean point that certain sentences only express a meaning which is truth-valuable 'when taken in conjunction with their context of utterance'; for it is only then that indeterminacies of sentence meaning are resolved. That Lemmon believes that the distinction between sentence meaning and sentence output sense is merely superficial is shown by his claim that 'the distinction is only worth upholding . . . in connection with those sentences whose truth-value *is* contextually dependent'.[7]

To begin with, we can ask: on what grounds, and with what justification do such philosophers say the meaning of a sentence like 'I am hot' is *indeterminate*? Certainly the sentence can be understood by any native speaker of English; it can be translated into other languages—and translated, moreover, without any suspicion that there is here such vagueness, ambiguity, or incompleteness of meaning as would render such a translation a mere approximation or guess. Of course, the reference of its putatively referring part, and hence its truth-value, are undetermined; but then these are no part of its sense! And, indeed, anyone who understands the sentence thereby *knows* that the sentence does not even purport to say who is hot, or when, or where, or how hot, etc. As Wittgenstein rightly observed: 'A proposition may well be an incomplete picture of a certain situation, but it is always a complete picture of *something*.' (*TLP*.5.156; cf. *PI*.§99.) What might with greater propriety be called 'indeterminateness of sense' is manifest by sentences which are ambiguous, sentences whose meaning (or meanings) is unclear, and not by sentences which do not, 'by themselves', determine a truth-value. The meaning of a sentence is determined by the meanings of its component expressions (*PSI*), and it is this which makes the meaning or input sense of a sentence independent of contextual factors. If we make the harmless but simplifying assumption that meanings do not

[7] Op. cit., p. 99.

change with time, then we can say that the meaning of the sentence 'I am hot' was the same yesterday as it is today, and as it was last century, irrespective of who uttered it, and where. On the other hand, the output senses which this sentence was or might have been intended to express will have differed on almost every occasion of its use. But what of such a sentence as, to use Lemmon's example, 'Brutus killed Caesar'? This sentence contains no token-reflexive elements, and therefore might seem to be 'true for all time'. Strangely enough, Lemmon himself provides the answer to this question, even though he contradicts himself in so doing. The sentence 'Brutus killed Caesar', he says, is to be considered true for all time only because 'most contemporary contexts would disclose that the reference of the two proper names "Brutus" and "Caesar" were well known Romans of that name'.[8] What Lemmon is alluding to here is the fact that there is no general linguistic rule to the effect that one and only one object shall be assigned a given proper name. But this means that the context is *always* relevant to the determination of output sense; and this is enough to establish the universal validity of the distinction between input and output sense, i.e. between what a sentence means, and what it *says* in a given context.

Summary: The distinction between the notion of input sense and that of output sense has been grounded in the following four asymmetries:

(1) Output sense is essentially sentential, whereas input sense (as employed, e.g. in *PS1*) is not.

(2) Output sense is sensitive to failure of reference, whereas input sense is not. (Hence input sense alone is incapable of determining a truth-value.)

(3) The notion of indeterminacy does not apply to input sense in the way in which it applies to output sense. In the former case it is equivalent to ambiguity.

(4) Input sense is not contextually dependent; output sense is.

4. OUTPUT SENSE AND THOUGHT

In the light of the foregoing, we may now establish certain conclusions concerning the two principles *PS1* and *PR2*. *PS1* is now seen to be true only if the word 'sense', in both its occurrences, is construed as signifying *input sense*. For it is true neither that sentence input

[8] Op. cit., p. 99.

sense nor that sentence output sense is determined by component output sense (there is no such thing as 'component output sense'); nor is it true that sentence output sense is determined by component input sense (as the context of utterance is also always a crucially determining factor). The second principle, *PR2*, on the other hand, must be read as relating the concepts *truth-value* and *output sense*; for as we saw above, mere input sense is incapable of either possessing or determining a truth-value. In short: there is no univocal sense of 'sense' which will satisfy both Frege's principles.

How serious a modification does this necessitate to Frege's theory of judgement? For Frege the objects of thought, as well as the primary bearers of truth-value, are *Gedanken*. And *Gedanken* are the senses of indicative sentences. But in what sense of 'sense' can this doctrine still be maintained? It seems clear that, whatever else the objects of thought are, (i) they are possible bearers of truth-value (otherwise we could not talk, as we wish to, of 'true beliefs', 'false judgements', 'the confirmation of suspicion', etc.), (ii) they are essentially expressible and communicable in language, and (iii) they are not, we have suggested, meanings or input senses, but claims or statements. The notion of *output sense* fulfils all three requirements. But before we may presume that we are possessed of a cogent and useful modification of Frege's theory, we must examine in greater detail the notion of output sense and discover if it will do the work required of it.

First, we might note, briefly, that the distinction between input sense and output sense provides us with a nice justification of the famous Fregean principle that a name only has reference in the context of a sentence.[9] Sub-sentential expressions, we have said, cannot express an output sense; but since input sense alone is incapable of determining a reference, it follows that sub-sentential expressions, in and of themselves, cannot be said to refer. They can, of course, be said to refer when they are used in a given proposition; but in this case it is their contribution to the total output sense which enables them to do this.

In 'Der Gedanke' Frege denies that any special sign marking the presence of assertive force is necessary in ordinary language: 'We

[9] 'Nur im Zusammenhange eines Satzes bedeuten die Wörter etwas' (*Gl.*73). Cf. M. D. Resnik, 'The Context Principle in Frege's Philosophy', *Philosophy and Phenomenological Research*, 27 (1967), 356–65; and 'Frege's Context Principle Revisited', in *Studien zu Frege*, ed. M. Schirn, Stuttgart, 1976, vol. III, pp. 35–49.

express the apprehension of a truth in the form of a declarative sentence. We do not need the word "true" for this; and even when we do use it, the real assertive force lies not in it, but in the form of the declarative sentence.' (*Ged*.62.) Now this would seem to imply that the utterance of a sentence in the indicative mood is, so to speak, naturally assertive: unless something intervenes to prevent an assertion from being made, then by simply uttering an indicative sentence one will be asserting that something is the case. This seems to be right. Not only are unqualified utterances considered assertive (pragmatically), but unembedded propositions in direct proofs in logic are considered assertive (logically). There are, however, as Frege points out, a number of types of occasion where this normal assertive force is cancelled. For example, an actor who, as part of a play, said 'This building is on fire', would not be taken to have asserted that the theatre is on fire. Nor would this have been asserted by someone who said 'If this building is on fire, I shall leave'. As Wiggins has observed: 'One might say that "*p*" automatically says that *p* unless you obstruct it from doing so.'[10] He further remarks that 'the common propositional content that "*p*" must really be got by subtraction from the assertion of "*p*", rather than from the latter by the addition of "⊢──" to "*p*"'. And this is, indeed, exactly the way in which Frege proceeded in the *Begriffsschrift* (cf. *Bs*.2–3). Now this is a deceptively important point. Formalists will perhaps argue that it makes little difference, if any, whether we regard assertive force as something which attaches to propositions or thoughts or, conversely, propositions and thoughts as abstractions from assertions. And as far as concerns the laying down of consistent rules for the use of the sign '⊢──' in a formal calculus, this is no doubt correct. On the other hand, if one is concerned with the philosophical analysis of the notions of judgement, thought, assertion, and the typical expressions which such acts receive in ordinary situations, then the differences between these two approaches become significant. Frege's naïve realism with respect to the entities he calls 'Thoughts', for example, can be traced to the *Grundgesetze* theory wherein '── ξ' denotes a concept, and '── $\varDelta$' an *object* to which assertive force may then be attached. In the *Begriffsschrift*, however, the notion of assertion was taken as primitive, and the content of an assertion (── $\varDelta$) was obtained from this by subtraction. But this earlier approach, by emphasizing that assertion is prior and that assertion is

[10] Loc. cit.

a human act, robs of plausibility the claim that there exist Thoughts prior to and independently of acts of thinking and judging. It is this that has enabled Thiel to call Frege's *Begriffsschrift* theory 'entirely Kantian'. The analysis of judgement according to the schema:

(4)   *agent + act + independent object*

is, in the *Begriffsschrift*, by no means inescapable or even attractive.

Frege's later epistemological theory is grounded in an ontological mystery concerning Thoughts. His account of judgement is, so to speak, transitive: adoption of schema (4) commits one to the view that where there is judging there exists something that is judged, just as where there is throwing there exists something that is thrown. We shall have to see how useful the hypostatization of such 'objects of thought' is in explaining the concept of judgement. But it is worth noting, first, that there is also an intransitive paradigm, to which Frege himself alludes in the *Logische Untersuchungen*—though without apparently feeling its attraction: 'We are probably best in accord with ordinary usage if we take a judgement to be an act of judging, as a leap is an act of leaping.' (*Vern.*151n.) This is right; but an act of leaping does not at all conform to schema (4). There are no 'leaps' which are autonomously existing entities which constitute the direct objects of acts of leaping. Certain human acts, that is, conform to the simpler schema:

(5)   *agent + act.*

Frege's motive for the adoption of schema (4) in his account of judgement was not, however, the result simply of ontological prejudice. On the contrary, he believed that only in terms of such a transitive account of judgement could the possibility of objectivity, of truth, be allowed for. He believed, that is, that abandonment of schema (4) would necessarily result in the subjectivization of judgement, so that judgements would become, like images, desires, and sensations, merely the contents of particular consciousnesses and not the objective bearers of truth-value. He thought that this would have the disastrous effect of reducing the truths of logic, mathematics, and science to 'a part of psychology'. He saw the contemporary move towards psychologism in science and idealism in philosophy as entirely pernicious: 'When will a stop be put to this? In the end everything is drawn into the sphere of psychology; the boundary that separates objective and subjective fades away more and more, and *even actual objects themselves* are treated psychologically, as ideas.' (*Gg*.xix) Now this last remark is revealing. Frege's paradigm of objectivity is an independently existing object or thing. It was natural, therefore, that in order to guarantee the objectivity of Thoughts he should have identified them with autonomous objects, albeit objects of a quite peculiar kind which inhabit the 'realm of sense'.[11] Nor did this ontologizing tendency stop here. In arithmetic, for example, not only was the Thought expressed by an equation an autonomous object, not only was the truth-value of such a Thought an autonomous object, but so too were the numbers themselves. These were the posts which Frege drove into ontology in order to halt the slide towards subjectivism.

This whole venture, I shall argue, is based on a misconception. It is based, that is, on the false dichotomy between what is ontologically autonomous and therefore objective, on the one hand, and what is merely subjective on the other. Kant was the first to recognize that not only is there a non-ontological, anti-realist means of protecting the objectivity of thought, knowledge, and science, but also that, in the last analysis, epistemological realism is necessarily unable to do this. The flaw in Frege's epistemology is not so much the falsity of the claim that Thoughts and truth-values are independently existing entities, but the failure of this hypothesis—whether true or not—to explain objectivity. The failure is this: The positing of an entity or entities (such as Thoughts) as the guarantors of objectivity is necessarily question begging, because we must have *objective knowledge of such entities*. Otherwise, as Kant observed, they would be as nothing to us. But, paradoxically, knowledge of such entities must be impossible; for otherwise we will need a warrant for the objectivity of such knowledge, and this leads to a vicious infinite regress. In other words, if some entity, T_1, is invested with the power of guaranteeing the objectivity of knowledge, no knowledge of T_1 will be possible. Advocates of epistemological realism have attempted to avoid this paradoxical conclusion by distinguishing between two kinds of knowledge: knowledge of facts (discursive) and knowledge of things (acquaintance). The regress is then avoided by showing that

[11] Frege himself, so far as I am aware, never calls Thoughts 'objects'. This was no doubt because to do so would have been to imperil the distinction between the 'realm of sense' and the 'realm of reference'. But this boundary is indefensible. Anyway, Thoughts are the references of complete expressions and ought therefore to be accorded the status of objects; certainly Thoughts are not functions.

discursive knowledge of some fact just *is* acquaintance with some entity T_1. It is then possible, the realist believes, either to deny outright that discursive knowledge of T_1 is possible, or, on the other hand, to admit that such knowledge is in a sense possible, but is to be analysed as acquaintance with some further entity T_2, which is some truth about T_1. But even brute acquaintance must involve the possibility of one's identifying and re-identifying these entities (cf. *Ged*.64), and this is a discursive ability which cannot be reduced to acquaintance. For if my ability to recognize T_1 as T_1 depends upon my acquaintance with T_2, which I identify as T_2 on the basis of my acquaintance with $T_3 \ldots$, then, again, a vicious regress ensues and objectivity becomes impossible. This is the case quite generally; that is, regardless of whether the entities in question are construed as 'facts', 'truths', 'existing states of affairs', or Fregean 'Thoughts'.

There are two aspects to the problem of the objectivity of judgement: one is the problem of *communication*, of how two or more people can think and say the same things, and know that they do so; the other is the problem of the *truth* of what they say and think. I shall argue that the hypostatization of Thoughts is unnecessary in either case. Thoughts can therefore be excised from our ontology with the help of Occam's Razor.

If it is the independent existence of a certain Thought that is to warrant the claim that two or more people can think the same thing, or mean the same thing by what they say, then there must be a means of identifying and re-identifying this Thought independently of such thinkings and sayings. Otherwise there is no ground for asserting that the Thought exits *independently*, and it can be unproblematically construed as a projection of, or abstraction from, such human activities. Yet such means are entirely lacking. I do not know that I understand my interlocutor on the basis of my having successfully identified, independently of his verbal and other behaviour, the Thought he is entertaining with the Thought I am entertaining. Frege himself admits that Thoughts can only be produced in public in linguistic guise (*Ged*.66n.), but fails to see clearly that this effectively prevents the notion of a Thought from performing one of the functions for which it was invented, namely explaining how objective communication is possible. In fact, however, Frege eventually has to resort to an act of faith (*Ged*.74) in order to overcome the sceptical doubt that he rightly sees is suggested by his doctrine: 'Is it at all the *same* Thought which first that man expresses and now this one?' (*Ged*.66). But as the notion of a Thought was introduced in part to explain *how* two people can express the same thing, we are justified in dismissing the notion as without function in such a theory.

The second aspect of this problem concerns, not the expressing or understanding of information, but its truth or falsehood. And here we come to one of the most popular and traditional arguments for platonic realism. 'Only a sentence supplemented by a time indication and complete in every respect expresses a Thought. But this, if true, is true not only today or tomorrow but timelessly.' (*Ged*.76.) It is true that the sun is larger than the earth, say, or that $2+2 = 4$; but these would be the case, Frege contends, even had there been no thinking beings to apprehend them, or any language in which to express them: 'Thoughts can be true without being apprehended'. He compares the scientist, whose task it is to establish and collate true Thoughts, with the geographical explorer: neither creates the objects of his inquiry or deals with merely subjective facts; rather, each 'comes to stand in a certain relation . . . to what already existed beforehand'.

Frege's argument is as follows. (i) It is Thoughts (and not, for example, sentences or acts of thinking) that are the primary bearers of truth-value. (For the purposes of this argument it is immaterial whether truth-values are taken as properties of Thoughts or as their references.) (ii) It is true that, for example, $2+2 = 4$. (iii) This truth is timeless. (That is, it would still be the case that $2+2 = 4$, even had no one said or thought so.) (iv) Therefore Thoughts exist timelessly. Now we can agree that premisses (i) and (ii) are true, provided, of course, that the term 'Thought' is not interpreted in a way that would beg the question. Premiss (iii) can also be interpreted in an uncontentious way, i.e. in conformity with the parenthetical gloss. But in this case the conclusion simply does not follow. For (iv) to follow from the premisses, (iii) would have to be strengthened so as to make the contentious claim that some truths *exist* timelessly. But the question at issue is precisely whether or not acknowledging the 'timelessness' of certain truths commits us to the *existence* of timeless entities which they are, which they express, or to which they refer. So the argument is circular if (iii) is strengthened in this way, and it does not go through if it is not.

What exactly does it mean to assert that a truth is 'timeless'? What precisely *is* the uncontentious way of reading premiss (iii)? Two interpretations have been offered. The first is that the sense of certain statements does not in any way depend upon factors present in the context of assertion. I have raised certain objections to this thesis in the preceding section. The second, acceptable, interpretation of (iii) has been advanced by Dummett. It can be read, he maintains, as a denial that a double set of truth conditions are necessary for any given thought: 'If . . . a thought were to be regarded as something whose existence depends upon there being some actual language in which it could be expressed, or at least some intelligent being capable of grasping it, it would follow that there were two conditions for the statement ['2+2 = 4 is true'] to be true: first, that [2+2 = 4], and, secondly, that there should be such a thing as the thought [that 2+2 = 4], i.e. that there should be a language in which that thought could be expressed or a being who was capable of grasping it.' (*FPL*.370.) Assertion of the 'timeless' truth of certain statements in (iii) above can, then, be construed as rightly denying that such statements have a double set of truth conditions. But, as Dummett further remarks, there is *nothing* in this thesis which would further commit us to timeless entities, the existence of which would constitute fulfilment of truth conditions of the first, proper kind.

We are free, therefore, to reject the realist assumptions embodied in schema (4) and to search for a more acceptable, intransitive alternative.

5. HISTORICAL NOTE

One objection which we have levelled against any theory of judgement which conforms to schema (4), namely that it is based upon an inappropriate linguistic paradigm, is usually associated with the later writings of Wittgenstein. It was he who gave most forceful expression to the claim that certain problems in philosophy are created *ex nihilo*, so to speak, by our failure to perceive properly the way in which language works, by our tendency to assimilate fundamentally different locutions to one and the same paradigm, and by our tendency to posit an entity corresponding to any substantive expression. Frege's theory of judgement commits all these sins. It is surprising to learn, therefore, that in the last years of his life Frege came to accept a position not dissimilar to that of Wittgenstein. In the private diary which Frege kept during 1924, the year of his death, his thoughts turned to the analysis of arithmetical statements which he had first propounded thirty years earlier, and which Russell had shown to be untenable. And he concluded that the surface forms of language had led him astray:

My efforts to get clear about what one wants to call a number have ended in failure. One is far too easily misled by language . . . The sentence 'six is an even number' . . . seems comparable to 'Sirius is a fixed star' . . . in which an object should be represented as falling under a concept. And so the words 'six', 'five' etc. seem to be proper names of objects . . . Thus it appears that the problem is to produce the object which appears to be signified by numerical words and signs.

And on the following day he wrote:

From the first lesson on, we are so used to employing the word 'number' and the numerals that we don't really consider any justification of these uses necessary . . . But with longer concern with this matter one comes to suspect that it is the use of language which leads one astray; that the numerals are absolutely *not* proper names of objects; and words like 'number', 'square root' and the like are *not* concept words. So that a sentence like 'four is a square number' does not express the subsumption of an object under a concept. And so this sentence cannot at all be construed like 'Sirius is a fixed star'. But then, *how*? (*Nach.*282.)

Unfortunately Frege never answered this question; nor did he, so far as we know, apply this line of reasoning to other forms of expression of interest to philosophers. Had he done so, many of the criticisms of his account of judgement offered in the preceding pages would have been rendered superfluous.

6. PHENOMENOLOGICAL NOTE

That (a) sentence utterances are naturally assertive (i.e. assertive until proved otherwise), and that (b) thoughts are not independent objects to which assertive force may be attached, these are theses which have interesting analogies in the phenomenological sphere. One such has been mentioned by Geach. 'It is possible', he writes, 'that a thought is assertoric in character unless it loses this character by occurring only as an element in a more complicated thought.'[12] And he adds: 'this would be a neat solution to the problem of how thought is related to judgement'. Now Geach is here maintaining the validity of the distinction between assertive and unassertive occurrences of thoughts (mental acts) directly analogous to the distinction

[12] P. T. Geach, 'Assertion', p. 457.

between assertive and unassertive occurrences of propositions in logic (see above, Chapter III, Section 3). The conventions governing propositions which occur in a direct proof is that all free-standing, unembedded propositions are assertive; embedded propositions, on the other hand (with the exception of the conjuncts of a conjunction) occur without assertive force. In our earlier examination, however, we decided that, *pace* Geach, this is not the only way in which linguistic phenomena may manifest or be without assertive force. A proposition which occurs within an indirect proof, for example, does not occur assertively; yet as Lewis Carroll's paradox shows, the occurrence of the proposition within the proof cannot be construed as a form of propositional embedding. There is, moreover, a pragmatic dimension to assertion which does not correspond to the former, logical dimension. These facts count against Geach's assimilation of the mental to the logical, and against his conclusion that a thought is assertoric 'unless it occurs only as an element in a more complicated thought'. For surely one can simply grasp a thought, without necessarily asserting it.

I believe we can approach closer to the phenomenological facts if we say that thoughts *naturally* occur assertively when they do not occur as part of a more complex thought. In other words it is not inevitable that a thought should occur assertively, but it is usual that it should. And by 'natural' I mean that an *additional* act is necessary if its assertiveness is to be cancelled. Judgements are phenomenologically basic; and the formulation of a hypothesis, or the suspension of judgement as to the truth of a given claim, these are to be regarded as subsequent, modificatory acts. This is not surprising. The thoughts which normally occur to us concern matters which we hope or fear, expect or intend, infer or believe, and do not occur to a truly disinterested mind prepared to abstain from judgement as to their truth.

The thesis that thoughts naturally occur assertively, and that an additional act, the suspension of judgement, is usually necessary if this force is to be cancelled seems, then, to be confirmed by the phenomenological evidence. There is, however, a logical reason why this should be so. If thoughts naturally occurred or were apprehended unassertively, an extra act of assertion or affirmation would be necessary in order to transform the thought into a judgement. But this act would itself be a judgement that the thought was true (or false). But if thoughts occur unassertively, the thought of the truth (or falsity) of the first thought would also occur without assertive force, and so would itself need to be judged to be true. And so if judgement is to be possible at all, it must be possible for some thoughts to occur assertively; and phenomenologically speaking, we can say that they normally do so.

7. 'CONCEPT CARRIED CONNECTEDNESS'

I have chosen as the title of this section a phrase used by Strawson in talking about Kant's theory of concepts and judgements.[13] I have done so because it seems to me that the phrase highlights one of the more fundamental philosophical motives which have led philosophers to take an interest in the phenomenon of judgement. It is, to put it crudely, in and through our ability to judge, to subsume objects under concepts, to assert that things are thus and so, that we make sense of the world. It is in judgement that order is brought to chaos and unity imposed on the disparate and divergent elements of experience. This 'connectedness' of experience, however, as Kant clearly saw and as Strawson has recently emphasized, is not a function of judgements of unity, that is of judgements which employ the concept

( ) *is a unity.*

Rather, it is a function of the unity of judgement, the puzzling phenomenon we mentioned in the Introduction to this work. And clearly there can be no explanation, not viciously circular, of the latter phenomenon in terms of the former.

Now it was in connection with the unity of judgement that Frege introduced and, even in the face of the gravest difficulties, continued to insist upon the 'unsaturated' nature of concepts. It is only, he claimed, because they are essentially incomplete that they *can* combine with objects so as to form an integral unity, and not remain simply an aggregate of independent elements. And although this doctrine did not enable Frege, in the last analysis, to give an account of propositional unity, at least it enabled him to take account of it, and so avoid the logical tangles which enveloped, for example, Russell and Moore. Russell found that his analysis was quite incapable of accounting for propositional unity: 'A proposition has a certain indefinable unity, in virtue of which it is an assertion; and this is so completely lost by analysis that no enumeration of constituents will restore it, even

---

[13] P. F. Strawson, *The Bounds of Sense*, pp. 110, 117.

though itself be mentioned as a constituent. There is, it must be confessed, a grave logical difficulty in this fact, for it is difficult not to believe that a whole must be constituted by its constituents.' (*PMs.* 466f.) Moore too found himself in difficulties over this very point. In his article 'On the Nature of Judgement' he, like Frege, asserts that a concept is neither a material or perceptible object, nor a mental or subjective idea: 'Concepts are possible objects of thought . . . It is indifferent to their nature whether anybody thinks them or not. They are incapable of change; and the relation into which they enter with the knowing subject implies no action or reaction.'[14] A proposition, Moore claims, is composed of concepts. But this leads him, inevitably, to ask 'wherein a proposition differs from a concept'. And his answer is that the difference between a concept and a proposition, 'in virtue of which the latter alone can be called true or false, would seem to lie merely in the simplicity of the former'. But, it must be asked, if concepts and propositions are entities belonging to the same logical type and differing only in degree of complexity, how can a 'simple' proposition like

This rose is red

be true or false, while a 'complex' concept like

( ) *is the dog that bit the cat that killed the rat that ate the grain that fed the mouse that lived in the house that Jack built*

cannot be either true or false? Something, one wants to say, is missing from the concept (however 'complex') which is necessarily present in the proposition (however 'simple'); and the nearest we have come so far to identifying this something is to say that it consists in a certain completion or saturation. Can we be more explicit?

We have already seen that Frege subscribed during the *Grundgesetze* period to what might be called a double jigsaw theory of propositional unity: a truth-value is composed (in the simplest case) of a complete object and an incomplete concept; a Thought (again in the simplest case) is composed of the sense of a complete expression and the sense of an incomplete expression. We have also seen that there is reason enough to reject, virtually lock, stock, and barrel, the jigsaw theoretical approach to propositional unity as far as concerns the 'realm of reference'. And we have also objected to Frege's jigsaw

---

[14] G. E. Moore, *Mind*, vii (1899). (Cf. Frege's almost identical pronouncements at *Ged.*76f.)

account of sentential sense, at least in so far as this involves the hypostatization of saturated and unsaturated entities which somehow come together, without human intervention, to form Thoughts. We must now attempt to formulate a non-ontological interpretation of the metaphor of 'saturation' as it applies to the notion of *sense*.[15] Wittgenstein was exercised by just this problem in the *Tractatus*, and an examination of his views will prove instructive; for they are in large part a development of some of Frege's most central theses.

The problem as Wittgenstein saw it, is to explain why a proposition is not a mere motley of words; 'for in a printed proposition, for example, no essential difference is apparent between a propositional sign and a word' (3.143).[16] Now in his concept-script Frege in fact made no typographical distinction between names of objects and sentences. The sign '*Δ*' as it occurs in '⊢——— *Δ*', say, could stand with equal propriety either for the person *Julius Caesar* or for the truth *that Julius Caesar is now dead*. In contrast Wittgenstein's proposed perspicuous notation would make such syntactical indeterminacy impossible. For reasons which need not concern us here, Wittgenstein believed that a language, any language, the propositions of which can stand in determinate logical relations one with another, is only possible if these propositions express a determinate sense. The search for the conditions—ontological, epistemological, and semantic —which must obtain if determinateness of sense is to be possible occupies much of the *Tractatus* and essentially involves the programme of logical analysis whereby (it is claimed) every meaningful proposition is in principle decomposable into so-called 'elementary propositions' and their truth-functional relations. An elementary proposition consists entirely of names which are primitive, indefinable signs whose sole semantic function is to refer to simple objects. The names which comprise an elementary proposition, in other words, do not express a sense.

This rather obscure and prima facie implausible programme is of interest in the present context for the following reason: it is in the notion of an elementary proposition that we meet in what must surely be its purest form the problem of propositional unity. An

---

[15] The failure of Frege's ontological account is, perhaps, sufficient to motivate the search for a non-ontological alternative. Arguments are presented below, however, in support of the claim that such an account must *necessarily* be non-ontological or anti-realist.

[16] Citations of references to the *Tractatus* will henceforward be simply numerical.

elementary proposition consists entirely of names. How, then, can it express a unary sense, a thought? Why is it not at best a list, at worst a mere agglomeration of senseless signs? By posing the problem in this form the inquiry is deepened in two ways. In the first place we cannot, with Frege, simply construe sentential sense as a function of the senses of the component sub-sentential expressions; for all such expressions are names and hence, for Wittgenstein, senseless. And, secondly, another approach to the problem is usefully blocked: we can no longer account for propositional unity in terms of the coming together, jigsaw-like, of 'saturated' and 'unsaturated' parts; for an elementary proposition consists of homogeneous elements, names.

All of this might well seem to contravene not only the letter but also the spirit of Frege's theory. And yet, that Wittgenstein will eventually provide a solution which is in all important respects Fregean is indicated by his adopting two of Frege's most fundamental insights: first that 'only in the context of a proposition does a name have meaning' (3.3); secondly, that 'wherever there is compositeness, argument and function are present' (5.47). Our problem is to show (a) how senseless names can come together to express a complete sense, and (b) how function and argument can be present in what looks, for all the world, like a string of names. In fact, as will emerge, these questions comprise but one problem—the answer to either is at the same time the answer to the other. To show how a proposition has sense is to show how it is a unity, and vice versa.

We can best begin by examining Wittgenstein's notion of an *Urbild* or proto-picture:

If we turn a constituent of a proposition into a variable there is a class of propositions all of which are values of the resulting variable proposition. . . . But if all the signs in it that have arbitrarily determined meanings are turned into variables, we shall still get a class of this kind . . . It corresponds to a logical form—a logical proto-picture. (3.315.)

Wittgenstein is here adopting a procedure for the generation of sentential function-names which is essentially Fregean, although variables are now employed instead of empty brackets as gap-holders. Thus what Wittgenstein (very misleadingly) calls a 'variable proposition' is merely a predicate. Suppose, then, that we turn all the constituents of a proposition, say 'Fa', into variables, then there results the proto-picture 'ϕx'. Frege himself called such an expression an 'unequal-levelled function-name' and, interestingly, anticipated

Wittgenstein by observing that it represents without restriction 'the relation which an object has to a concept under which it falls' (*Gg*.§22). Now Frege is undoubtedly right that 'ϕx' is unequal-levelled: it contains a place not only for a singular term, but also for a first-level function-name. It seems therefore that it cannot be an *elementary* proto-picture; for as such it would have to consist entirely of individual variables. Wittgenstein, however, failed notoriously to provide an example of a primitive name, or an elementary proposition, or an elementary proto-picture. But let us suppose that the signs 'A', 'B', and 'C' are in fact primitive names, and that

(6)   ABC

is an elementary proposition, the immediate concatenation of three senseless but referring signs. In this case the corresponding proto-picture will be:

(7)   *xyz*

or, under the alternative and, I think, more perspicuous Fregean convention:

(8)   [ ] ( ) { }.

At the deepest level of analysis, the *Tractatus* picture theory claims that the relations in which names stand to one another within an elementary proposition represent or portray, via a rule of projection, the way in which the objects referred to by those names stand to one another in a possible state of affairs. But the relation in which the names stand to one another in a proposition is exactly what the corresponding proto-picture is designed to exhibit. Wittgenstein's proto-pictures are generated in the same way as Frege's function-names, by the successive removal of component names from a complete expression; but in the former case *all* the component expressions are names. What Wittgenstein has shown is that even in this limiting case 'function and argument are present'. The elementary proto-picture, in representing the form of an elementary proposition, is performing the same semantic role as a predicate does in an ordinary sentence. In other words, if (6) asserts that B is between A and C,[17] then the proto-picture (7) (or (8)) is performing the role normally performed by the more familiar predicate expression

[17] If, in fact, (6) did assert this, then it could not for Wittgenstein be elementary, as it would not be independent of all other elementary states of affairs. This, however, is a complication we can ignore in the present context.

(9)   ( ) is between [ ] and { }.

Given a rule of projection which entitles us to interpret the spatial relations in (8) as possible relations between objects, then we can assert that certain objects *are* so related by concatenating their names in the pattern given by (8). We can, then, read Wittgenstein quite literally when he writes that a proposition is 'a *function* of the expressions contained in it' (3.318). But note that there is now no temptation to construe the function as a part or component of the propositional whole: (8) simply does not occur in (6). Moreover just the same account can be given of the more familiar predicate expression (9) and its role with respect to the sentence

(10)   B is between A and C.

Wittgenstein himself makes this point at 3.1432.

This, at last, gives us a non-metaphorical acocunt of the property of being 'unsaturated', at least as this applies to expressions. Both a sentence and a name are actually *expressions*, i.e. self-subsistent objects whose criteria of identity are typographical; a predicate, on the other hand, is not an expression at all, but rather the *form of an expression*. And as such it is clearly not complete in itself but is, precisely, the form *of* something.[18]

At this point we can say that the unity and completeness manifested by an elementary proposition are a result of its exhibiting a form which conforms to a rule of projection. Wittgenstein has reinterpreted Frege's static, jigsaw account of functions as 'unsaturated entities' dynamically: functions become rules for the meaningful concatenation of expressions. So now all our problems concerning the unity of judgement are concentrated in the notion of a rule of projection; and indeed the remainder of this work will be devoted to an examination of this difficult and elusive concept. A rule of projection, at this point, just is whatever it is that enables a concatenation of expressions to express a complete thought.

8. THE PRINCIPLE OF IMMEDIACY

According to the *Tractatus*, the putting together of expressions according to a rule of projection will only express a sense if those expressions themselves have reference (*Bedeutung*). Thus if (6) is to express a thought *two* conditions must be met: (8) must be a pattern

[18] See above, Chapter I, §5.

to which there corresponds a rule of projection; and 'A', 'B', and 'C' must be signs with *Bedeutung*. The possibility of significant 'pictorial form', that is, depends upon the obtaining of the 'pictorial relation' which links each pictorial element (or name) with some extra-pictorial (extra-linguistic) object. These links, Wittgenstein wrote, 'are, as it were, the feelers of the picture's elements, with which the picture touches reality' (2.1515). But, and this is the problem, the possibility of there being a 'pictorial relation' depends in its turn upon there being significant 'pictorial form'. Only if each pictorial element or name is linked to an extra-pictorial object can the elements come together to express a thought; but this correlation or linking is something that can only occur *within* a propositional context (3.3). We cannot, that is, construe the activity of formulating a proposition as the bringing together of elements which *already* stand correlated with objects. The creation of pictorial form, on the one hand, and of the pictorial relation, on the other, must occur simultaneously. And how this can happen is, to say the least, problematic.[19]

One of the central claims of the *Tractatus*, we have seen, is that if picturing is to be possible at all, there must be a link or tie between the elements of the picture and the elements of the state of affairs depicted. But, on pain of vicious infinite regress, *this link cannot itself be pictorial*. The feelers which the picture's elements put out must, so to speak, make immediate, direct contact with reality. It is this thought which underlies Wittgenstein's argument for the existence of simple objects which are linked with semantically simple signs:

Objects make up the substance of the world. That is why they cannot be composite.

If the world had no substance, then whether one proposition had sense would depend on whether another proposition was true.

In that case we could not sketch out any picture of the world (true or false). (2.021ff.)

If the relation between a given pictorial element and the extra-pictorial object which is its *Bedeutung* were not immediate, then the possibility of there being any depiction of a state of affairs at all would depend upon the obtaining of that mediating state of affairs governing this relation. So whether one proposition had sense would depend upon whether another proposition were true; but if this were always the case a vicious regress would prevent there being

[19] Cf. 3.263.

any connection between picture and depicted state of affairs, between language and reality. The simplicity of objects and the senselessness of primitive names is the form which this requirement of non-pictorial immediacy takes in the *Tractatus*. And given that sense be determinate this is quite right: 'the requirement that simple signs be possible is the requirement that sense be determinate' (3.23). Objects are simple and their names are senseless—this is, for Wittgenstein, the guarantee that an immediate connection between language and reality is possible; for such names *can* only be immediately linked with such objects. If the names had sense, then they would be pictorial, and if the objects were complex, then the sense of any proposition containing their names would be indeterminate.

Unfortunately this doctrine left Wittgenstein with a considerable problem as to how the immediate correlation between name and simple object is set up, recognized, or maintained. Clearly this link cannot be set up *outside* a propositional context because baptism is itself a form of discursive activity. But its happening *within* a proposition is something that Wittgenstein himself later described as 'occult'. Even in the *Tractatus* the tension at just this point makes itself felt. Considering the problem how one can know with what a given name has been correlated, Wittgenstein wrote:

The meanings of primitive signs can be made clear by means of elucidations. Elucidations are propositions that contain the primitive signs. So they can only be understood if the meanings of those signs are *already* known. (3.263, my italics.)

If we take this literally, it implies that unless one already knows what a given primitive name refers to, then one never will. The dilemma is as follows: either the name/object relation is immediate and ineffable, in which case communication would seem to be impossible, or, on the other hand, the relation can be elucidated, in which case it is in some sense propositional and hence not immediate. But the latter alternative would break the link between language and the world— a link which it is precisely the aim of the *Tractatus* theory to forge. And so with complete consistency, Wittgenstein rejects this alternative and embraces the linguistic solipsism which emerges at 5.62.

So far I have considered the Principle of Immediacy (as I shall call it) only as it is employed in the *Tractatus* where, because it is wedded to the requirement of the determinateness of sense, it leads to fairly disastrous results. But the principle is in no way dependent on this requirement; indeed, it is strengthened when we drop it. Quite generally, if discursive thought is to be possible then, sooner or later, there must be some immediate, non-discursive link between the thought and what it is about. At some point in our theory, that is, we must be able to say '*That* is how thought (or language) is attached to reality; it reaches right out to it' (cf. 2.1511). Kant was, I believe, the first to perceive this clearly:

If understanding in general is to be viewed as the faculty of rules, judgement will be the faculty of subsuming under rules. . . . But if it is sought to show in general *how* we subsume under rules, that is, how we distinguish whether something does or does not come under them, then that could only be by means of another rule. This in turn, for the very reason that it is a rule, again demands guidance from judgement. (*B*.171f.)

The vicious regress which results from a denial of the Principle of Immediacy leads Kant to posit what he calls 'the spontaneity of judgement'. This is a power of synthesis which according to Kant is 'blind but indispensable'. Now, as we shall see in a moment, the 'blindness' of this power is one of the most central issues in Wittgenstein's later philosophy. We can, however, note here—as a first approximation—that the power of judgement must ultimately be blind because, as Kant points out in the above passage, the only possible candidate for guide is judgement itself.

We have already noted in connection with the *Tractatus* picture theory the manifold difficulties engendered by the necessarily non-propositional means by which we identify the object referred to by a given proper name. The same problem resurfaces in the *Philosophical Investigations*, this time in connection with the meanings of words for sensations. How, Wittgenstein asks, can one come to learn to use the name of a particular sensation correctly? And he answers: 'What I do is not, of course, to identify my sensations by criteria, but to repeat an expression' (*PI*. §290). And this, he continues, is something that I do 'without justification'. To deny this is to accept that whether one proposition has sense will depend upon whether another proposition is true. For the sense of the sentence containing the name of a sensation would depend upon whether the sensation has been identified correctly. If a vicious infinite regress is to be avoided, if language and thought are to be possible at all, then there must be a point at which language and thought make immediate contact with reality; and here 'immediate' means non-criterial, non-judgemental.

The application of the Principle of Immediacy to judgements concerning sensations in the *Investigations* is, however, merely one particular application of quite general conclusions which Wittgenstein reaches concerning what it is to follow or obey a rule. Like Kant, Wittgenstein asks 'How am I able to obey a rule?' And, like Kant, his answer is ultimately 'blindly': 'When I obey a rule I do not choose. I obey the rule blindly' (*PI.* §217f.). Now the notion of blind obedience is not an attractive one, and it can easily seem that Wittgenstein is here maintaining a thesis which is either just empirically false (that we can never enter into rational deliberation as to whether we will or will not act in conformity with a given rule) or morally reprehensible (that one's obedience to established practice ought to be unquestioning). His point, however, is neither empirical nor moral. It is a logical point about the form which any coherent *theory* of judgement must take. Any theory, that is, which demands that judgement must or may always precede adoption of a rule is incoherent. In particular it is incoherent with respect to precisely those fundamental rules (rules of projection) which make thought, rational deliberation, and judgement themselves possible. Rules of projection, conformity to which is a necessary condition of a proposition's having a sense at all, are not rules which can be examined, chosen, or rejected without our *already* acting in conformity with such rules. And this is why Wittgenstein's account of what it is to follow a rule in general terminates in the notion of a *custom* or *practice*. The Principle of Immediacy demands that in the last analysis the notion of a rule must be non-discursive, non-propositional; otherwise the Kantian vicious regress ensues to make judgement impossible. Wittgenstein gives what is, I think, appropriately bizarre expression to this truth when he says 'You can't get behind the rules, because there isn't any behind' (*PG.*244).

It is necessary, I think at this point to guard against a possible misinterpretation. Nothing I have said commits me to the absurd claim that one cannot judge, think about, choose to act or not to act in conformity with a given rule. Wittgenstein is wrong, that is, to suggest that all rules are followed blindly; but he is right to insist that if any rules are to be followed at all, then *some* must be obeyed blindly. This is a truth which no theory of judgement can ignore.

Fundamental rules of projection, then, are arbitrary: no philosophical justification or explanation can be given of them. But, *a fortiori*, no ontological justification or explanation can be provided for them.

Yet this is exactly what Frege's post-*Grundlagen* theory of judgement attempted to provide. According to Frege, a judgement is a complete, unitary act because, finally, a truth-value is a complete unitary *object*. The sense or content of a judgement is determined by its truth-conditions which are simply the conditions under which that judgement would refer to just that object. But if I am right, then no realist account of the unity—and hence of the significance—of judgement is possible. The Principle of Immediacy would seem to be compatible only with an anti-realist account of human thought and language. The unity of judgement cannot, as Kant saw, be explained by appeal to the prior and independent notion of the unity possessed by an object—regardless of whether that object is a material particular, a Thought, a fact, or a truth-value. For Kant, the categories, the rules which govern the creation of propositional unity, are nothing more than 'concepts of an object in general, by means of which the intuition of an object is regarded as determined in respect of one of the logical functions of judgement' (*B*.128f.). In other words, while it is in principle possible to define the ontological concept *object* in terms of the epistemological concept *judgement*, the reverse procedure is impossible, for it contravenes the Principle of Immediacy. Something of this truth is captured by the traditional definition of an object as what can be the subject, but never the predicate of a judgement. Frege himself at times subscribes to an account of this kind (e.g. at *Gl*.77n.); but then his subsequent appeal to objects in order to explain, in their turn, the unity and significance of judgement is blatantly and viciously circular.

Any acceptable philosophical account of human judgement must have a terminus. But for obvious reasons that terminus cannot be, or presuppose, those very discursive abilities which were to be elucidated. And so our ability to think, to judge, to manipulate concepts depends upon our performing acts which are essentially non-conceptual, and which are, therefore, inaccessible to philosophical analysis or investigation. These acts are nevertheless performed in conformity to rules. For the author of the *Tractatus* the point of immediate contact between judgement and the world is the relation between a senseless name and a simple object. For the author of the *Philosophical Investigations*, on the other hand, this requirement of immediacy is met by the possibility of our learning to follow a rule without *already* being able to follow a rule. One's behaviour can conform to a given rule—and this behaviour can be learned—without its being the case that certain conditions are judged satisfied, or that certain behaviour is judged called for on the part of the person acquiring the ability.[20] Kant expressed this succinctly: 'judgement is a peculiar talent which can be practised only and cannot be taught. . . . Examples are thus the go-cart of judgement' (*B*.171f.).

The terminus of the theory, then, is that point at which conceptual analysis gives way to brute facts. 'Brute' because such data must be incapable of philosophical analysis or explanation. There can no more be a philosophical account of how we are able to follow a rule in general than there can be a philosophical account of the human digestive process: both are non-conceptual, non-discursive processes. At this point one's philosophical spade is turned. Kant, having argued that the categories are the fundamental rules governing the creation of propositional unity, observes that 'this peculiarity of our understanding, that it can produce *a priori* unity of apperception solely by means of the categories, and only by such and so many, is as little capable of further explanation as why we have just these and no other functions of judgement' (*B*.146). All we can say here is: this is what we do.

9. CONCLUSION

Our conclusion is that a judgement is a mental act, specifically an internalized assertion, whose significance and unity are functions of its being performed according to a rule or rules of projection. In the simplest case this involves the assertion that an object falls under a concept, or that a concept falls within a higher level concept—and this, at least, has a Fregean ring to it. But, in general, with what justification can the theory we have defended be called Fregean?

There are, I think, four major strands to Frege's theory of judgement:

I. There is the methodological principle that 'we can distinguish parts in the thought corresponding to the parts of a sentence, so that the structure of the sentence serves as a model of the structure of the thought' (*Gef*.36).

II. A thought is (a) objective, (b) the sense of an indicative sentence, and (c) an autonomously existing entity.

[20] Since writing this it has been brought to my attention that J. Hintikka makes a similar point in his essay 'Language-Games', in *Acta Philosophica Fennica*, 28, nos. 1–3 (1976), 110–11.

III. A thought must have at least one 'unsaturated' or functional element, otherwise its elements would fail to coalesce and would remain merely disparate atoms.

IV. In a thought (a) the complete elements refer (if at all) to objects and (b) the unsaturated elements refer (if at all) to concepts or functions.

The position I have attempted to defend in this book is in substantial agreement with all these Fregean theses, with the exception of II(c) and IV(b). I have suggested that the hypostatization neither of 'Thoughts' as the denizens of a 'realm of sense' nor of concepts as the 'unsaturated' denizens of a 'realm of reference' is needed in order to account for either the unity, the significance, or the objectivity of judgement. The objectivity of a judgement is a function of the objectivity of the rules according to which it is formulated; and these rules have been classified under the notions of *syntax*, *input sense*, and *output sense*. But in thus rejecting the ontological underpinnings of Frege's theory we have been forced to move from what I earlier characterized as a mundane position to a transcendental one. And this necessitated a reinterpretation of the central Fregean notions of *sense*, *unsaturatedness*, *reference*, and *function*. This reinterpretation, it transpires, has consequences which are unavoidably anti-realist.

What Kant attempted to capture in his theory of the spontaneity of the activity of synthesis, what motivated Wittgenstein's *Tractatus* theory of the concatenation function exhibited in an elementary proto-picture, as well as his later account of what it is to follow a rule, and what, with a certain amount of charity, we can say lay behind Frege's insistence upon the 'unsaturatedness of concepts' was one and the same fundamental intuition: a judgement is an act, the act of putting together tokens (whether physical, psychical, or linguistic) in conformity with certain rules. It is in terms of such rules that the most basic aspects of the phenomenon of judgement are to be explained; and it is in the notion of a rule that the philosophical analysis of judgement comes to an end.

APPENDIX

FREGE'S PHILOSOPHY OF ARITHMETIC

In the preceding text reference has occasionally been made to Frege's doctrines concerning the concept *number* and the foundations of mathematics in general, to Russell's Paradox and the *coup de grâce* which its discovery delivered to Frege's system. What follows is intended as a brief—and relatively uncontroversial—introduction to such matters as these, which, although not an essential part of Frege's theory of judgement, nevertheless comprise the doctrinal and methodological background against which it was formulated.

1. *The logicist programme*

Both as a professional mathematician and as a philosopher Frege considered it scandalous that the foundations of 'the most exact of all the sciences', mathematics, should be treated in the cursory and superficial manner virtually universal amongst those of his contemporaries who even concerned themselves with such foundations at all. Nor, with the possible exceptions of Kant and Leibniz, did Frege find in the history of philosophy much that was valuable in this respect. He embarked, therefore, upon a programme of investigation which was designed to fulfil two basic theoretical needs: to *explain the concepts*, and to *secure the truths* of arithmetic and analysis.

The first of these aims needs little explanation and no justification. Questions such as 'What are numbers?', 'What do arithmetical propositions assert?', 'What is the logical form of ascriptions of number?' and the like express problems central to the philosophy of mathematics—a discipline which, indeed, came of age in the works of Frege. Regardless of the specific answers which he provided to them, we can say that Frege had every right to ask such questions as these. 'If a concept fundamental to a mighty science gives rise to difficulties, then it is surely an imperative task to investigate it more closely until those difficulties are overcome.' (*Gl*.ii.) Frege found such difficulties in the concept *number*. His avowed intent to justify or secure the truths of arithmetic, on the other hand, may well strike one as somewhat anachronistic, if not downright immodest. Arithmetic, it might with some justification be maintained, not only ought to be, but in fact is, well able to stand on its own feet: judgement as to its validity can hardly be suspended until such time as the philosopher has awarded his imprimatur. Nevertheless, historical considerations enable us to see why this objective was as important for Frege as was the other.

Frege saw his task as, in part, the protection of the objectivity, universality, and necessity of arithmetical truth against subversive and pernicious attacks. These attacks were of three main sorts: (i) Psychologism in science and idealism in philosophy which, Frege believed, would reduce the concept *true* to that of *believed to be true*, and hence result in the subjectivization of all science, including mathematics. (ii) 'Formalism', a doctrine according to which numbers are to be identified with numerals (signs), and the truths of arithmetic with the rules for the manipulation of such signs and the consequences of such rules. This, for Frege, would trivialize arithmetic so that it would become merely an arbitrary and conventional game, ultimately of no more importance than, say, chess. (iii) Any theory which, like empiricism, construes number as a property of objects, or a property of collections of objects. Such theories, Frege argued, not only fail to account for the logical form of statements of number (see below), but also tend to identify the truths of arithmetic with empirical, inductively based generalizations. All three alternatives were canvassed at the time Frege was writing; and all three failed, he maintained, either because they were unable to account for the necessity and/or objectivity of arithmetical truth, or because they were unable to recognize the deep logical differences between the ascription of a property to an object, and the ascription of a number.[1]

Frege's own programme, which became known subsequently as 'logicism', essentially involves establishing (i) that the primitive concepts of arithmetic and analysis are logical concepts, i.e. that numbers, arithmetical functions, and operations can be reduced to, or defined exclusively in terms of, purely logical notions; and (ii) that the truths of arithmetic are logical truths, analytical statements which can be known *a priori*. 'In arithmetic we are not concerned with objects which we come to know from without through the medium of the senses, but with objects given directly to reason and, as its nearest kin, utterly transparent to it. And yet, or rather for that very reason, these objects are not subjective fantasies. There is nothing more objective than the laws of arithmetic.' (*Gl.*115.)

Numerals and number-words may occur in two different types of sentential context, Frege maintained; he called them respectively ascriptions of number (*Zahlangaben*), and propositions of arithmetic (*arithmetische Sätze*). An ascription of number is a statement which provides an answer to the question: 'How many . . . ?'. 'There are three coins in the fountain', 'The population of London is twelve million', 'Jupiter has four moons', 'There are no windows on the ground floor' are all such ascriptions of number. On the other hand, however, there are propositions of

---

[1] For Frege's attack on psychologism see *Gl.*33–8, *Gg.* Introduction, and Review of Husserl's *Philosophie der Arithmetik*; for his assault on formalism: *Gg.*ɪɪ, §§86–137; and for his objections to empiricism: *Gl.*9–12 and 29–32.

arithmetic, such as 'Two is an even prime', 'Three is a square root of nine', and '2+5=7'.

'But when we make an ascription of number', Frege asks, 'what do we ascribe the number *to*?' (*Gl.*58.) His justly famous answer is that an ascription of number expresses an assertion about a concept (*Gl.*59, *Gg.*ix). Here number is not a property of objects, or of collections of objects, but rather a property of concepts: a second-level concept within which first-level concepts are said to fall.[2] Thus to say that there are three coins in the fountain, for example, is to assert of the first-level concept

(ξ) *is a coin in the fountain*

that it has this property (i.e. that it falls within this second-level concept):

has three instances.

This analysis is given considerable plausibility by Frege's observations that, in the first place, neither the coins themselves individually, nor the group of coins as a whole can be that to which the number three is ascribed; for there is *one* group, and it is made up of *single* coins. Secondly, Frege observes that one cannot simply point at something and ask 'How many is *that*?'. The only sensible response to a question of this sort is to ask in return 'How many *what*?'. But this is merely to request the (first-level) concept to which a number may be ascribed. A third consideration which Frege adduces in support of his analysis of the logical form of ascriptions of number is that only in this way can an account of the number zero be provided which is commensurate with the account given of the other, positive numbers. 'If I say "Venus has 0 moons", there simply does not exist any moon or agglomeration of moons for anything to be ascribed to. What happens, however, is that a property is assigned to the *concept* "moon of Venus", namely that of including nothing under it.' (*Gl.*59.) And finally, as the last quotation indicates, the logical form of ascriptions of number is assimilated to that of quantificational statements. This has great plausibility; for statements about 'all ϕs', 'some ϕs', and 'no ϕs' are shown to be of the same fundamental form as those about 'two ϕs', 'a hundred ϕs', and the like. And this possession of a common underlying form is nowhere more apparent, as Frege himself remarks (*Gl.*65), than in the case of the number 0: 'An assertion of existence is nothing more than denial of the number nought', and, conversely, a denial of existence is merely an ascription of the number nought.

In a proposition of arithmetic, on the other hand, such as 'two is an even prime', the number-word or numeral does not appear to play an ascriptive or attributive role, but functions rather as a singular term. Put very crudely we might say that here we are not predicating two of something, but predicating something of two itself. Frege maintained that in an

[2] See above, Chapter I, §5.

arithmetical proposition numerals occur as the proper names of *objects* (numbers), and not merely as signs comprising parts of second-level function-names. '2 is an even prime' thus asserts of the object

the number two

that it falls under the first-level concept

(ξ) *is an even prime.*

Numerical objects are for Frege, of course, neither material, perceptible objects existing in space, nor mental, subjective entities existing only in or for consciousness. 'Number words are to be understood as standing for self-subsistent objects' (*Gl*.73), albeit abstract or logical objects which are accessible only to reason. And having construed numbers as objects, Frege then consistently asserts that arithmetical equations are in fact identity statements. '2+5=7', for instance, asserts that the object referred to by the expression '2+5' is none other than the object referred to by the expression '7'.

Now in the *Grundlagen* there is some tension between the claim, on the one hand, that numbers are self-subsistent *objects* and, on the other hand, that an ascription of number involves an assertion about a *concept*. At times Frege seems to maintain that the prior, theoretically primitive phenomenon is the independent existence of mathematical objects: 'we should not be deterred by the fact that in the language of everyday life, number also appears in attributive constructions. *That* can always be got round.' (*Gl*.69.) And yet at other times he seems to deny this: 'The self-subsistence I am claiming for number is not to be taken to mean that a number word signifies something when removed from the context of a proposition, but only to preclude the use of such words as predicates or attributes, which appreciably alters their meaning.' (*Gl*.72.) This same tension is observable also in Frege's vacillation over whether a given number is to be defined as a concept, or as the extension of a concept (an object). In the *Grundlagen*, that is, Frege identifies numbers with objects that are the extensions of concepts—yet in the very passage in which this identification is effected he adds 'I believe that for "extension of a concept" we could simply write "concept"' (*Gl*.80n.); and in the conclusion to the work he remarks that 'I attach no decisive importance even to the bringing in of extensions of concepts at all' (*Gl*.117).

Some nine years later, in the *Grundgesetze*, this tension has all but vanished, and the analysis of numbers identifies them with the extensions of concepts (or *Wertverläufe*). But, in view of the difficulties which this identification creates (see below), it is worth noting that even in the later work Frege does express some reservation concerning such extensions and the way in which they are introduced: 'A dispute can arise, so far as I can see, only with regard to my Basic Law (V), concerning *Wertverläufe*, which logicians perhaps have not yet expressly enunciated, but which is what people have in mind when, for example, they speak of the extensions of concepts.' (*Gg*.vii.) This difficult (and for Frege disastrous) issue is taken up again in section 3 below.

2. *The cardinal numbers*

Having provided an account of the logical form of both ascriptions of number and propositions of arithmetic, Frege next turns to the cardinal numbers themselves. It is in this context that he propounds the important and historically influential maxim that, in a scientific language 'if we are to use the symbol *a* to signify an object, we must have a criterion for deciding in all cases whether *b* is the same [object] as *a*' (*Gl*.73). As *Zahlangaben* involve the ascription to a given concept of a number, the requirement that there be identity conditions for numbers is equivalent to the demand that we have a precise specification of the truth-conditions of sentences of the form:

the number which belongs to the concept *F* is the same as the number which belongs to the concept *G*,

whatever the concepts *F* and *G* might be. Such an account must fulfil two general conditions: it must not, on pain of circularity, make any appeal to such notions as *number* or *the number which belongs to a concept*; and, secondly, if it is to constitute a part of the reduction of arithmetic to logic, then the terms in which it is couched must be purely logical terms. This is effected as follows.

When two or more events occur at the same time we say they are simultaneous; when two points are the same distance apart as two other points we say they are equidistant. In the same way we can introduce a (technical) term for the relation in which two or more concepts stand to one another when the same number of objects falls under each: let us say they are 'equinumerous' (Frege's word is *Gleichzahlig*). If, for instance, there are exactly as many knives on the table as there are plates, then the two concepts (ξ) *is a knife on the table* and (ξ) *is a plate on the table* are equinumerous. The problem now is to provide a logical definition of this concept. Like Hume before, and Russell after him,[3] Frege achieves this by appeal to the notion of a one-to-one correspondence between the objects falling under the one concept and the objects falling under the other concept:

. . . if a waiter wishes to be certain of laying exactly as many knives on a table as plates, he has no need to count either of them; all he needs to do is to lay immediately to the right of every plate a knife, taking care that every knife on the table lies immediately to the right of a plate. (*Gl*.81–2.)

---

[3] D. Hume, *Treatise*, Bk.ı, part iii, §1, and B. Russell, *PMs*.113f.

Here it is the spatial relation

(ξ) *is to the immediate right of* (ζ)

which correlates one-to-one the knives and the plates on the table; which shows, that is, that the two concepts (ξ) *is a knife on the table* and (ξ) *is a plate on the table* are equinumerous. Can we, then, provide an exact definition of 'equinumerous', employing the notion of a one-to-one relation, in exclusively logical terms? We can, as follows: two concepts F and G are equinumerous just in case there is some relation, R, such that

(i) $(x) \{Fx \supset (\exists y)(z)[Gy \quad \& \quad (xRz \equiv z = y)]\}$

and

(ii) $(y) \{Gy \supset (\exists x)(z)[Fx \quad \& \quad (zRy \equiv z = x)]\}.$

This provides us with an exactly specified equivalence relation (*having the same number as*) which has been defined without any recourse either to the concept *number*, or to the individual numbers themselves (not even the number one).

The individual cardinal numbers Frege next proceeds to introduce by a process known as 'abstraction'. This warrants the move from an equivalence relation (holding in this case between concepts) to an identity holding between objects.[4] Thus from the statement

(1)   concept F is EQUINUMEROUS WITH concept G

we move to a statement about objects (numbers):

(2)   the number belonging to concept F is IDENTICAL
          WITH the number belonging to concept G.

In other words we transform (1), a statement of equivalence (equinumerosity), into (2), a statement of strict identity, by introducing abstract objects (numbers) of which this identity is to hold. In the move from (1) to (2), Frege says, 'we carve up the content in a way different from the original way, and this yields us a new concept' (*Gl*.75); in this case it is the concept of numbers as objects.

This procedure, whereby an equivalence relation is transformed into an identity, is not restricted to logic and mathematics. As Frege points out,

[4] An equivalence relation is any relation R which is transitive, symmetrical, and reflexive. In other words, if R is a first-level relation, then for all objects x, y, and z, the following must hold:

(i) $(xRy \ \& \ yRz) \supset xRz$
(ii) $xRy \supset yRx$
(iii) $(\exists y) xRy \supset xRx.$

(It should be noted that the process referred to here is quite distinct from 'Lockean abstraction', about which Frege is highly critical, see *Gl*.44–7.)

it is such abstraction which entitles us to take seriously as objects such things as shapes and directions. If, for example, it is the case that

(3)   line *a* IS PARALLEL TO line *b*,

then, by 'carving up the content in a different way', we can say

(4)   the direction of *a* IS IDENTICAL WITH the direction of *b*.

And in (4) we are asserting the numerical identity of objects (directions), something which is justified by the fact that parallelism is an equivalence relation. In a similar way it is the possession of the equivalence relation of equinumerosity which justifies the introduction of numbers by abstraction —though numbers, unlike directions, are introduced by abstraction on an equivalence relation between concepts.

The provision of truth-conditions for statements of the form:

the number which belongs to the concept *F* is the number which belongs to the concept *G*

does not yet tell us what a number *is*. We still, that is, need an account of expressions of the form:

(5)   the number which belongs to the concept *F*.

Frege provides what is, in effect, a stipulative definition: expressions such as (5) are to be interpreted as synonymous with those of the form:

(6)   the extension of the concept *equinumerous with the concept F*.

The justification of this stipulation lies in the fact that if concepts *F* and *G* are equinumerous, then the extensions of the two concepts *equinumerous with F* and *equinumerous with G* are identical. Numbers, it transpires, are extensions of equinumerous concepts.

It remains, now, to introduce and define the individual numbers themselves (0, 1, 2 . . . etc.). Again, this must be achieved with the aid of logical tools and procedures only. The cardinal number zero Frege defines by appealing to an arbitrarily chosen, but necessarily empty concept—a concept, that is, which as a matter of logical necessity has nothing falling under it. Frege chooses the concept

( ) *is not identical with itself.*

And so the number zero, the number which necessarily belongs to the concept *not identical with itself*, Frege defines as

the extension of the concept *equinumerous with the concept: not identical with itself.*

This is the result of applying the rule of transition, i.e. from statements of the form (5) to those of the form (6), to the true statement

0 is the number belonging to the concept *not identical with itself*.

Frege then generates the infinite series of natural numbers by demonstrating the universal warrantability of the move from any natural number n to its successor $(n+1)$. Specifically this is achieved by appeal to the fact that the number which belongs to the concept:

member of the series of natural numbers ending with n

is itself $(n+1)$, i.e. follows immediately in the series after n (*Gl*.94; *Gg*.100). So, incorporating the foregoing definition of zero, we can generate the natural numbers as follows:

$0 =$ the extension of the concept *equinumerous with the concept: not identical with itself*

$1 =$ the extension of the concept *equinumerous with the concept: identical with 0*

$2 =$ the extension of the concept *equinumerous with the concept: identical with 1 or 0*

   ... and so on.

3. *Russell's Paradox*

In the *Grundgesetze* Frege gave a formal presentation of the doctrines already defended informally in the *Grundlagen*, and attempted to develop these doctrines further.[5] The earlier work had established merely as a 'very probable conclusion' that the truths of arithmetic are analytic and *a priori* (*Gl*.118). In order to establish this conclusion beyond mere probability, Frege embarked upon an ambitious programme designed to derive the fundamental truths of arithmetic from just six basic laws or axioms expressing logical truths. In June 1902 the second volume of the *Grundgesetze* was already at the printer's and Frege believed that his programme had been fully implemented, when he received a short, friendly letter from the young Bertrand Russell. The letter led him to see that the theory of concept extensions upon which his whole programme was based was inconsistent. Russell wrote:

There's only one point about which I have difficulty. You assert ([*Bs*.] p. 17) that functions can also comprise indeterminate elements. I used to believe this; now, however, this view seems doubtful to me because of the following contradiction. Let ω be the predicate: is a predicate which cannot be predicated of itself. Can one predicate ω of itself? From either answer the opposite follows. And so one must conclude that ω is not a predicate at all. (*Brief*.211.)

Likewise, Russell adds, there can be no class (C) whose members are those classes which do not include themselves. For it could be asked of C:

[5] There is some debate amongst Fregean scholars as to the precise degree to which the theories of the *Grundlagen* and the *Grundgesetze* overlap. This, however, is an issue which it would be inappropriate to pursue here.

Does it include itself? If it did, then it would have to possess the defining characteristic of members of that class—in other words it would not belong to itself. But if, on the other hand, C was not a member of itself then it would belong to the class of classes which do not belong to themselves—in which case it would belong to itself. Frege's system, that is, allows the derivation of the following contradiction:

$$C \in C \equiv C \notin C.$$

In fact, Russell's Paradox as it applies to concepts and predicates does not infect Frege's system; for a predicate expression cannot occur in the argument-place of a predicate expression of the same level. Fregean categorial grammar makes the result syntactically malformed. The Paradox as it applies to classes (extension, sets, *Wertverläufe*, etc.), however, strikes at the very foundations of Frege's work—for he had identified numbers with the extensions of concepts.

Now Frege nowhere specifies exactly how he understands the expression 'extension of a concept', or the closely related term *Wertverlauf*, a somewhat striking omission given the crucial role performed by these notions in his theory. Two general points can be noted immediately, however: first, an extension is a 'proper' object; secondly, it is a necessarily *abstract* object. As a proper object an extension is a proper argument for any first-level function. This, as we shall see, creates problems. The necessarily abstract nature of the extension of a concept, say $\phi(\xi)$, is sufficient to distinguish it from the composite whole which comprises the totality of objects which fall under it. The whole or *manifold* which has as its parts the objects which fall under $\phi(\xi)$ will be a concrete object if the objects themselves are concrete. Now there are, as Frege argued against Schröder (*KBS*.436f.), a number of difficulties which attach to the notion of a manifold and which make it an unsuitable concept upon which to base an account of number. Because a manifold is articulated in terms of its *parts*, it is difficult (a) to distinguish the manifold which corresponds to a concept from the object which falls under that concept, in the case where, as a matter of fact, only one object does fall under it; (b) to acknowledge 'an empty manifold', for a manifold must 'vanish when the objects [which compose it] vanish. If we burn down all the trees in a wood, we thereby burn down the wood'; and (c) to attach a unique number to a manifold. Because the parts of parts of a manifold are also parts of the manifold, manifolds can be arbitrarily divided into parts. 'But an object to which I can ascribe different numbers with equal right is not what really has a number.' (*Gl*.29.) (Subsequent work, especially by Leśniewski, has tended to show that Frege's rejection of 'manifold-theory' was, at least, premature. But in Frege's favour it can be said that while his objections to such an approach are not, perhaps, final, the points he raises represent real difficulties with which the whole/part theorist must come to terms.)

So Fregean conceptual extensions are not manifolds in the foregoing sense. What, then, are they? A partial answer to this question can be given by showing how extensions are introduced into Frege's system, and by providing identity conditions for them. Frege calls the extension of a concept the *Wertverlauf* of that concept,[6] and he introduces into the symbolism of the *Grundgesetze* a special notation for such objects. Their names are formed as follows: the letter (e.g. 'ξ') which holds open the argument-place in a function-name is replaced by a lower-case Greek vowel enclosed in brackets. The whole thus formed is then prefixed by that same Greek vowel with a smooth breathing ('). And so the name for the *Wertverlauf* which corresponds to the concept $\phi(\xi)$ is written

$$\grave{\epsilon}\phi(\epsilon)$$

while that of the non-sentential function $\xi+2$ is

$$\grave{\alpha}(\alpha+2).$$

But of course merely stipulating a procedure for the transformation of expressions of one sort into those of another does not yet constitute an acceptable means of introducing the *Wertverläufe* themselves. This latter task Frege accomplishes by means of abstraction. If two concepts, say $\phi(\xi)$ and $\psi(\xi)$, stand in the equivalence relation

always have the same value for the same argument

then, Frege says, the *Wertverläufe* of the two concepts are identical. In other words, if

(7) $\underline{\quad\quad\underset{\smile}{\alpha}\quad\quad}\ \phi\,(\alpha)=\psi(\alpha)$

then

(8) $\grave{\epsilon}\phi(\epsilon) = \grave{\alpha}\psi(\alpha).$

The equivalence relation (7) which holds between first-level concepts is the basis for the introduction of the identity (8) which holds between objects. This is incorporated into one of Frege's Basic Laws of the *Grundgesetze*; in fact, the notorious Basic Law (V):

(V) $\vdash\!\!\!\underline{\quad}(\grave{\epsilon}f(\epsilon)=\grave{\alpha}g(\alpha))=(\underline{\quad\quad\underset{\smile}{\alpha}\quad\quad}f(\alpha)=g(\alpha))$

---

[6] *Wertverlauf* (plural *Wertverläufe*) is sometimes translated as 'value-range' or 'course-of-values'; but as neither of these translations is ideal and both are as unwieldy as the original, I prefer to leave the term untranslated.

It is from this axiom that Russell's Paradox can be derived.[7]

Axiom (V) provides identity conditions for *Wertverläufe*. But as we noted earlier, the mere provision of identity conditions does not yet tell us *what it is* that is, under such and such conditions, identical. Nor is it in this respect informative to stipulate that a *Wertverlauf* just is an object introduced by abstraction on a given equivalence relation. So far 'we have only a means of always recognizing a *Wertverlauf* if it is designated by a name like '$\acute{\epsilon}\phi(\epsilon)$' ... But we can neither decide, so far, whether an object is a *Wertverlauf* that is not given as such, and to what function it may correspond, nor decide in general whether a given *Wertverlauf* has a given property.' (*Gg*.16.)

Now it has been convincingly argued that a straightforward identification of Fregean *Wertverläufe* with Russellian classes is mistaken.[8] For Russell and many others, the extension of the concept, say,

(9)   (ξ) *is an author of Principia Mathematica*

encompasses just two objects: A. N. Whitehead and B. Russell. The extension of this concept is the class of authors of *Principia*, and this class has just two members. Frege, in contrast, gives the following hint as to what he takes *Wertverläufe* to be:

The method of analytic geometry supplies us with a means of intuitively representing the values of a function for different arguments. If we regard the argument as the numerical value of an abscissa, and the corresponding value of the function as the numerical value of the ordinate of a point, we obtain a set of points that presents itself to intuition (in ordinary cases) as a curve. Any point on the curve corresponds to an argument together with the associated value of the function. (*FuB*.8; cf. *Gg*.5.)

This analogy would suggest that the *Wertverlauf* of a concept is not the Russellian class of objects falling under it, but rather the totality of values as determined by the totality of possible arguments. Thus the *Wertverlauf* of concept (9) will be comprised of those ordered couples, one for each and every object, the first member of which is the object and the second member of which is the value of the concept for that object:

> A. N. Whitehead; the True
> Genghis Kahn; the False
> The number 3; the False
> B. Russell; the True
> $\acute{\epsilon}\phi(\epsilon)$; the False
> ... and so on, for all the objects there are.

[7] The closest Russellian approximation to (V) is:

$$\hat{x}f(x) = \hat{x}g(x) \ . \ \equiv \ . \ (x)(f(x) \equiv g(x)).$$

[8] See, e.g., R. S. Wells, 'Frege's Ontology', reprinted in *Klemke* (particularly

The self-referentiality which lies at the root of Russell's Paradox is, incidentally, already evident here. For if we identify $\grave{\epsilon}\phi(\epsilon)$ with the *Wertverlauf* of the concept (9), then we have a concept which must be defined for an object which that concept itself is subsequently used to introduce.

Contradiction arises in Frege's system in the following way. Axiom (V) asserts that when the *Wertverläufe* of any two concepts are identical, then any and every object which falls under either concept also falls under the other. But *Wertverläufe* themselves are also objects; so concepts must be defined for them too as arguments. But it follows from (V) that for any object *a*, and any concept $\phi(\xi)$, if ϕa then *a* occurs in the extension of $\phi(\xi)$. (In other words, the ordered pair $\langle a;$ the true$\rangle$ occurs in the *Wertverlauf* whose name is '$\grave{\epsilon}\phi(\epsilon)$'.) This Frege expresses by the unrestricted assertion that for any object *a*:

$$(10) \qquad \qquad \vdash\!\!\!\!\!-\, f(a) = a \cap \grave{\epsilon}f(\epsilon)$$

But, on the supposition that '*a*' denotes the extension of the concept

(11)   (ξ) *is the extension of a concept under which it does not fall,*

while '$f(\xi)$' denotes (11) itself, we immediately obtain Russell's Paradox.

'Hardly anything more unwelcome can befall a scientific writer', Frege wrote in a hastily added appendix to the second volume of the *Grundgesetze*, 'than that one of the foundations of his edifice be shaken after the work is finished.' In this appendix Frege tried to assess and repair the damage which Russell's discovery had inflicted, an attempt which has come to be known subsequently as 'Frege's way out'.[9] The trouble, we have said, is caused by Axiom (V). More specifically, it is caused by the unrestricted adoption of the principle of class abstraction, according to which there corresponds to every first-level function an object which is its extension.[10] Precisely what Russell's letter showed was that this correspondence does not always hold. Some restriction must, therefore, be placed on

pp. 13–16); and M. Furth, 'Editor's Introduction' to G. Frege, *The Basic Laws of Arithmetic*, p. xxxviii.

---

[9] For example: W. v. O. Quine, 'On Frege's Way Out', reprinted in *Klemke*, 485–500; P. T. Geach, 'On Frege's Way Out', reprinted in *Klemke*, 502–4; and M. D. Resnik, 'Some Observations Related to Frege's Way Out', *Logique et analyse*, 7 (1964), 138–44.

[10] Hereafter the differences between Fregean *Wertverläufe* and Russellian classes cease to be significant.

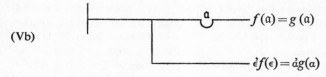

(Vb)

for it is this (equivalent to the left-to-right reading of (V)) that legitimizes unrestricted class abstraction. Frege proceeded in what was, perhaps, the most natural manner. He restricted or weakened (Vb) so that the extension of a given concept encompasses all the objects falling under that concept, *with the exception of that extension itself* (*Gg*.II, 262). So, in order for some object a to be included in the extension of a concept $\phi(\xi)$ it must be the case that

$$a \neq \acute{\epsilon}\phi(\epsilon).$$

Frege's modified version of (Vb) is thus:[11]

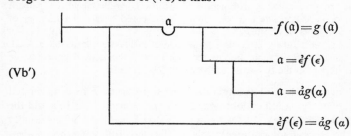

(Vb')

This restriction does, indeed, prevent Frege's system from yielding Russell's Paradox; unfortunately however, as thus modified the system is 'inconsistent in any universe of more than one member'[12]—a disastrous result for a system designed to provide a foundation for arithmetic.

Upon learning of Frege's proposed amendment Russell's immediate reaction was that 'it seems very likely that this is the true solution' (*PMs.* 522n.). But Russell quickly came to the conclusion that the true solution in fact lay elsewhere: in the direction of a theory of logical types. We noted above that the Paradox does not infect Frege's doctrine of concepts and functions. This is because the rules of syntax for the concept-script make it impossible for a function-name of any given level to occupy the argument-place of a function of that same level: the paradox simply cannot be formulated. There is, thus, a hierarchy of functions: functions of objects

[11] In Russellian notation this would be written:

$\hat{x}f(x) = \hat{x}g(x) . \supset . (y)[(y \neq \hat{x}f(x) \quad \& \quad y \neq \hat{x}g(x)) \supset (f(y) \equiv g(y))]$

[12] The phrase is Quine's (op. cit., p. 492). The proof that this is the case was discovered, independently, by Leśniewski and Quine. For further details see works listed in n. 9 above.

(level-1); functions of first-level functions (level-2); functions of second-level functions (level-3), . . . and so on. Russell's own preferred solution was to introduce such a type hierarchy into the realm of classes. Thus while for Frege *all* classes are 'proper' objects, fit to be arguments in any first-level function, for Russell classes of objects were to be sharply distinguished from classes of classes of objects, classes of classes of classes of objects, . . . and so on. [13]

Now although he had long subscribed to what amounts to a theory of logical types for concepts and functions, Frege felt unable to extend such a hierarchical ordering to classes. This was partly because he believed that a class, being 'saturated', was necessarily an object, and hence of level-0 in a type hierarchy. More importantly, he also recognized that adoption of a type-theoretical approach to classes would prevent any *general* account of arithmetic from being formulated; for one would need to redefine the numbers afresh at each level:

> With this, the generality of arithmetical propositions would be lost. Again, it would be incomprehensible how on this basis we could speak of a number of classes or a number of numbers.
> I think this is sufficient to render this [type-theoretical] route impassable as well. There is no alternative at all but to recognize the extensions of concepts, or classes, as objects in the full sense of the word. (*Gg.*II, 255.)

This is not the place to examine the logicist programme as it developed after Frege, or the modifications which it must undergo if it is to avoid the paradoxes of set theory. But we can note that Frege himself eventually rejected the programme as unrealizable. In the years following the publication of the second volume of the *Grundgesetze* he came increasingly to hold a Kantian position, according to which arithmetical truths are not, after all, analytic but synthetic *a priori*. The *Nachlass* shows him attracted to the possibility of providing a geometrical rather than a logical foundation for arithmetic; and geometry had always been, for Frege, synthetic *a priori*. This new approach was not, however, implemented or examined in any great detail. As Dummett has observed, it is interesting 'chiefly as showing that Frege did, at least at the very end of his life, acknowledge the failure of the logicist programme . . . and had the energy to begin to construct an alternative whole theory of the foundations of mathematics to replace it' (*FPL.*664). Frege died in 1925 having neither repaired his original programme nor discovered an acceptable alternative.

But this failure, it must be noted, in no way detracts from the philosophical value of Frege's other theories; theories concerning, amongst others, the notions of *sense, concept, object, judgement*, and *thought* which it has been our aim to explore in the main body of this work.

---

[13] See, e.g., 'Mathematical Logic as Based on the Theory of Types', in B. Russell, *Logic and Knowledge* (ed. R. C. Marsh), pp. 59–102.

BIBLIOGRAPHY

PART I

AJDUKIEWICZ, K., 'On Syntactical Coherence', *Rev. Met.* xx (1967), 635–47. (Transl. by P. T. Geach.)

ANSCOMBE, G. E. M., *An Introduction to Wittgenstein's Tractatus*, London, 1959.

—— and GEACH, P. T., *Three Philosophers*, Oxford, 1961.

AUSTIN, J., *Philosophical Papers*, Oxford, 1961.

—— *How to do things with Words*, Oxford, 1962.

BARTLETT, J. A., 'On Questioning the Validity of Frege's Concept of a Function', *J. of Phil.* lxi (1964), 203.

BENNETT, J., *Kant's Dialectic*, Cambridge, 1974.

BLACK, M., *Problems of Analysis; Philosophical Essays*, Ithaca, 1954.

—— *Philosophy in America*, London, 1965.

—— 'Frege on Functions', in *Problems of Analysis;* reprinted in *Klemke*, pp. 223–48.

BRADLEY, F. H., *Appearance and Reality*, London, 1893.

—— *The Principles of Logic* (2nd edition), London, 1928.

CARNAP, R., *Meaning and Necessity*, Chicago, 1947 and 1956.

CARROLL, L., 'What the Tortoise said to Achilles', *Mind*, iv (1895), 278–80.

CARTWRIGHT, R., 'Propositions', in *Analytical Philosophy*, ed. J. R. Butler (1st Series), Oxford, 1962, 81–103.

—— 'Propositions Again', *Noûs*, ii (1968).

—— 'Some Remarks on Essentialism', *J. of Phil.* lxv (1968), 615–26.

CHURCH, A., 'On Carnap's Analysis of Statements of Assertion and Belief', *Analysis*, x (1950), 97–9.

—— 'A Formulation of the Logic of Sense and Denotation', in *Structure and Meaning: Essays in Honor of Henry M. Sheffer*, ed. P. Henle *et al.*, New York, 1951, pp. 3–24.

—— *Introduction to Mathematical Logic*, Princeton, 1956.

COPI, M., 'Objects, Properties and Relations in the *Tractatus*', *Mind*, lvii (1958), 145–65.

CROSSLEY, J. N. and DUMMETT, M. A. E. (edd.), *Formal Systems and Recursive Functions*, Amsterdam, 1965.

DAVIDSON, D., 'Truth and Meaning', *Synthese*, xvii (1967), 304–23.

—— 'True to the Facts', *J. of Phil.* lxvi (1969), 748–64.

—— 'On Saying That', in *Words and Objections; Essays on the Work of W. V. Quine*, ed. D. Davidson and J. Hintikka, Dordrecht, 1969, pp. 158–74.

DAVIDSON, D. and HARMAN, G. (edd.), *Semantics of Natural Language*, Dordrecht, 1972.

DUMMETT, M. A. E., 'Frege on Functions; a Reply', *Phil. Rev.* lxiv (1955), 96–107.

—— 'Note, Frege on Functions', *Phil. Rev.* lxv (1956), 229–30.

—— 'Nominalism', *Phil. Rev.* lxv (1956), 491–505.

—— 'Truth', *PAS* lix (1958), 141–62.

—— *Frege: Philosophy of Language*, London, 1973. See CROSSLEY, J. N.

FELDMAN, F., 'Sortal Predicates', *Noûs*, vii (1973), 268–82.

FREGE, G., *Begriffsschrift, eine der arithmetischen nachgebildete Formelsprache des reinen Denkens*, Halle, 1879.

—— *Die Grundlagen der Arithmetik: eine logisch-mathematische Untersuchung über den Begriff der Zahl*, Breslau, 1884.

—— *Funktion und Begriff*, Jena, 1891.

—— 'Über Sinn und Bedeutung', in *ZPK* (1892), 25–50.

—— 'Über Begriff und Gegenstand', in *VWP* xvi (1892), 192–205.

—— *Grundgesetze der Arithmetik. Begriffsschriftlich abgeleitet*, I, Jena, 1893.

—— Review of E. G. Husserl, *Philosophie der Arithmetik*, I, in *ZPK* (1894), 313–32.

—— 'Kritische Beleuchtung einiger Punkte in E. Schröders *Vorlesungen über die Algebra der Logik*', in *ASP* i (1895), 433–56.

—— 'Über die Begriffsschrift des Herrn Peano und meine eigene', in *BVK* xlviii (1897), 361–78.

—— *Grundgesetze der Arithmetik, Begriffsschriftlich abgeleitet*, II, Jena, 1903.

—— 'Was ist eine Funktion?', in *Festschrift Ludwig Boltzmann gewidmet zum sechzigsten Geburtstage, 20. Februar 1904*, Leipzig, 1904, pp. 656–66.

—— Notes to P. E. B. Jourdain on 'The Development of the Theories of Mathematical Logic and the Principles of Mathematics: Gottlob Frege', in *QJPAM* xliii (1912), 237–69.

—— 'Der Gedanke. Eine logische Untersuchung' *BPI* i (1918), 58–77.

—— 'Die Verneinung. Eine logische Untersuchung', *BPI* i (1918), 143–57.

—— 'Logische Untersuchungen. Dritter Teil: Gedankengefüge', *BPI* iii (1923), 36–51.

—— *Nachgelassene Schriften*, ed. H. Hermes, F. Kambartel, and F. Kaulbach, Hamburg, 1969.

—— *Wissenschaftlicher Briefwechsel* (*Nachgelassene Schriften*, Bd. II), ed. G. Gabriel, H. Hermes, *et al.*, Hamburg, 1976.

FURTH, M., 'Editor's Introduction', in G. Frege, *The Basic Laws of Arithmetic: see* Part II, below, p. 161.

—— 'Two Types of Denotation', in *Studies in Logical Theory*, ed. N. Rescher, Oxford, 1968, pp. 9–45.

GEACH, P. T., 'Quine on Classes and Properties', *Phil. Rev.* lxii (1953), 409–12.
—— 'Class and Concept', *Phil. Rev.* lxiv (1955), 561–70.
—— 'On Frege's Way Out', *Mind*, lxv (1956), 408–9.
—— *Mental Acts*, London, 1957.
—— 'Assertion', *Phil. Rev.* lxxiv (1965), 448–54.
—— *Reference and Generality* (emended edition), Ithaca, 1968.
—— *Logic Matters*, Oxford, 1972.
—— and BLACK, M. (edd. and transl.), *Translations from the Philosophical Writings of Gottlob Frege*, Oxford, 1952.
   See ANSCOMBE, G. E. M.
GRIFFIN, J., *Wittgenstein's Logical Atomism*, Oxford, 1964.
GROSSMANN, R., 'Frege's Ontology', *Phil. Rev.* lxx (1961), 23–40.
HARMAN, G., *Thought*, Princeton, 1973.
   See DAVIDSON, D.
HEIJENOORT, J. VAN, 'Logic as Calculus and Logic as Language', *Synthese*, 17 (1967), 324–30.
HEINZ, J., *Subjects and Predicables*, The Hague, 1973.
HINTIKKA, J., *Knowledge and Belief*, Ithaca, 1962.
—— *Models for Modalities*, Dordrecht, 1969.
—— *Logic, Language-Games and Information*, Oxford, 1973.
—— 'Language-Games', *Acta Philosophica Fennica*, 28, nos. 1–3 (1976), 105–25.
JOURDAIN, P., 'The Development of the Theories of Mathematical Logic and the principles of Mathematics: Gottlob Frege', in *QJPAM* xliii (1912), 237–69.
KANT, I., *The Critique of Pure Reason* (1st edn., Riga, 1781; 2nd edn., 1787). Translated (both editions) by N. Kemp Smith, London, 1929.
KLEMKE, E. D. (ed.), *Essays on Frege*, Urbana, 1968.
KNEALE, W. and M., *The Development of Logic*, Oxford, 1962.
KRIPKE, S., 'Naming and Necessity', in *Semantics of Natural Language*, ed. D. Davidson and G. Harman, Dordrecht, 1972, pp. 253–355.
LEMMON, E. J., 'Sentences, Statements and Propositions', in *British Analytical Philosophy*, ed. B. Williams and A. Montefiore, London, 1966, pp. 87–107.
LONG, P., 'Are Predicates and Relational Expressions Incomplete?', *Phil. Rev.* lxvii (1969), 90–8.
MARSHALL, W., 'Frege's Theory of Functions and Objects', *Phil. Rev.* lxii (1953), 347–90.
—— 'Sense and Reference: a Reply', *Phil. Rev.* lxv (1956), 342–61.
MOORE, G. E., 'The Nature of Judgement', *Mind*, vii (1899), 176–93.
PATZIG, G., *Sprache und Logik*, Göttingen, 1970.
PITCHER, G. (ed.), *Truth*, Englewood Cliffs, 1964.
PLATO, *Sophist*, in *The Dialogues of Plato*, ed. B. Jowett, Vol. III, Oxford, 1875.

PRIOR, A. N., 'Oratio Obliqua', *PAS* (Supp.) xxxvii (1963), 115–26.
—— 'Indirect Speech and Extensionality', *Phil. Studs.* 15, (1964), 35–8.
—— *Objects of Thought*, ed. P. T. Geach and A. Kenny, Oxford, 1971.
QUINE, W. V. O., 'Designation and Existence', in *J. of Phil.* xxxvi (1939), 701–9; repr. in *Readings in Philosophical Analysis*, ed. H. Feigl and W. Sellars, New York, 1949.
—— 'On Frege's Way Out', *Mind*, lxiv (1955), 145–59.
—— *Elementary Logic*, New York, 1965.
RAMSEY, F. P., *The Foundations of Mathematics and Other Logical Essays*, ed. R. B. Brathwaite, London, 1931.
RESNIK, M. D., 'Some Observations Related to Frege's Way Out', *Logique et analyse*, 7 (1964), 138–44.
—— 'Frege's Theory of Incomplete Entities', *Ph. of Sc.* 32 (1965), 329–41.
—— 'The Context Principle in Frege's Philosophy', *Philosophy and Phenomenological Research*, 27 (1967), 356–65.
—— 'Frege's Context Principle Revisited', in *Studien zu Frege*, ed. M. Schirn, Stuttgart, 1976, Vol. III, pp. 35–49.
RUSSELL, B., 'On Denoting', *Mind*, xiv (1905), 479–93.
—— *The Principles of Mathematics*, London, 1903.
—— *Principia Mathematica* (with A. N. Whitehead), Cambridge, 1910–3; 2nd ed 1925.
—— 'Mathematical Logic as Based on the Theory of Types', reprinted in *Logic and Knowledge*, ed. R. C. Marsh, London, 1956, pp. 59–102.
—— 'The Philosophy of Logical Atomism', in *Logic and Knowledge*, ed. R. C. Marsh, London, 1956, pp. 175–282.
RYLE, G., '"If", "So" and "Because"', repr. in *Philosophical Analysis*, ed. M. Black, Cornell, 1950, pp. 323–40.
SCHIRN, M. (ed.), *Studien zu Frege*, I–III, Stuttgart, 1976.
SCHWAYDER, D., 'Uses of Language and Uses of Words', *Theoria*, xxvi (1960), 31–43.
SEARLE, J., 'Russell's Objections to Frege's Theory of Sense and Reference', *Analysis*, xvii (1957), 137–43.
—— *Speech Acts; an Essay in the Philosophy of Language*, London, 1970.
SEUREN, P. A. M. (ed.), *Semantic Syntax*, Oxford, 1974.
SLOMAN, A., 'Functions and Rogators', in *Formal Systems and Recursive Functions*, ed. J. N. Crossley and M. A. E. Dummett, Amsterdam, 1965, pp. 156–75.
STRAWSON, P. F., 'Truth', *Analysis*, ix (1949), 83–97.
—— 'On Referring', *Mind*, lix (1950), 320–44.
—— *Introduction to Logical Theory*, London, 1952.
—— *Individuals; an Essay in Descriptive Metaphysics*, London, 1959.
—— 'Singular Terms and Predication', *J. of Phil.* lvii (1961), 393–412.
—— *The Bounds of Sense*, London, 1966.
—— (ed.), *Philosophical Logic*, Oxford, 1967.

—— *Meaning and Truth*, Oxford, 1970.

—— *Subject and Predicate in Logic and Language*, London, 1974.

SUMMERS, F., 'Predicability', in *Philosophy in America*, ed. M. Black, London, 1965, pp. 262–81.

TEICHMAN, J., 'Propositions', *Phil. Rev.* lxx (1961), 500–17.

THIEL, C., *Sinn und Bedeutung in der Logik Gottlob Freges*, Meisenheim Glan, 1967. (Transl. by J. Binkley, *Sense and Reference in Frege's Logic*, Dordrecht, 1968.)

WELLS, R. S., 'Frege's Ontology', *Rev. Met.* iv (1951), 537–73.

WHITEHEAD, A. N., *see* Russell, B.

WIGGINS, D., *Identity and Spatio-Temporal Continuity*, Oxford, 1967.

—— 'On Sentence Sense, Word Sense and Difference of Word Sense. Towards a Philosophical Theory of Dictionaries', in *Semantics. An Interdisciplinary Reader*, ed. D. D. Steinberg and L. A. Jacobovits, Cambridge, 1971.

WILSON, J. C., *Statement and Inference*, Oxford, 1926.

WILSON, N. L., *The Concept of Language*, 2nd edition, Toronto, 1959.

—— 'The Trouble with Meanings', *Dialogue*, iv (1964), 52–64.

WITTGENSTEIN, L., *Tractatus Logico-Philosophicus*, transl. D. F. Pears and B. F. McGuinness, London, 1961.

—— *Philosophical Investigations*, ed. G. E. M. Anscombe, G. H. von Wright, and R. Rhees; transl. G. E. M. Anscombe, Oxford, 1953, 2nd ed 1958.

—— *Remarks on the Foundations of Mathematics*, ed. G. E. M. Anscombe, G. H. von Wright, and R. Rhees; transl. G. E. M. Anscombe, Oxford, 1956.

—— *Notebooks, 1914–1916*, ed. G. H. von Wright and G. E. M. Anscombe; transl. G. E. M. Anscombe, Oxford, 1961.

—— *Philosophical Grammar*, ed. R. Rhees; transl. A. Kenny, Oxford, 1974.

PART II

SOME ENGLISH TRANSLATIONS OF FREGE'S WORKS

1879

Begriffsschrift, eine der arithmetischen nachgebildete Formelsprache des reinen Denkens
(a) partial transl. by P. T. Geach in *G&B*. 1–20.
(b) complete transl. by S. Bauer-Mengelberg, in *From Frege to Gödel, a source book in mathematical logic*, ed. J. van Heijenoort, Cambridge, Mass., 1967, pp. 1–82.

160 BIBLIOGRAPHY

(c) complete transl. by T. Bynum, in *Conceptual Notation and related articles*, ed. T. Bynum, Oxford, 1972, pp. 101–203.

1882

'Über die wissenschaftliche Berechtigung einer Begriffsschrift'
(a) transl. by J. M. Bartlett, as 'On the Scientific Justification of a Concept-script', in *Mind*, lxxiii (1964), 155–60.
(b) transl. by T. Bynum, as 'On the Scientific Justification of a Conceptual Notation', in *Conceptual Notation and related articles*, ed. T. Bynum, Oxford, 1972, pp. 83–9.

1883

'Über den Zweck der Begriffsschrift'
(a) transl. by V. H. Dudman, as 'On the Purpose of the *Begriffsschrift*', in *Australasian Journal of Philosophy*, xlvi (1968), 89–97.
(b) transl. by T. Bynum, as 'On the Aim of the "Conceptual Notation"', in *Conceptual Notation and related articles*, ed. T. Bynum, Oxford, 1972, pp. 90–100.

1884

Die Grundlagen der Arithmetik. Eine logisch-mathematische Untersuchung über den Begriff der Zahl
transl. by J. L. Austin, as *The Foundations of Arithmetic*, Oxford, 1959.

1891

Funktion und Begriff
transl. by P. T. Geach, as 'Function and Concept' in *G&B*. 21–41.

'Über das Trägheitsgesetz'
(a) transl. by R. Rand, as 'About the Law of Inertia', in *Synthese*, xiii (1961), 350–63.
(b) transl. by H. Jackson and E. Levy, as 'On the Law of Inertia', in *Studies in the History and Philosophy of Science*, ii (1971/2), 195–212.

1892

'Über Sinn und Bedeutung'
(a) transl. by H. Feigl, as 'On Sense and Nominatum', in *Readings in Philosophical Analysis*, ed. H. Feigl and W. Sellars, New York, 1949, pp. 85–102.
(b) transl. by M. Black, as 'On Sense and Reference', in *G&B*. 56–78.

'Über Begriff und Gegenstand'
transl. by P. T. Geach, as 'On Concept and Object', in *G&B*. 42–55.

1893/1903

Grundgesetze der Arithmetik. Begriffsschriftlich abgeleitet (vol. I, 1893; vol. II, 1903)
(a) partial transl. by P. E. B. Jourdain and J. Stachelroth, P. T. Geach and M. Black, in *G&B*. 137–244.
(b) partial transl. by M. Furth, *The Basic Laws of Arithmetic*, Berkeley and Los Angeles, 1964.

1894

Review of E. G. Husserl's *Philosophie der Arithmetik. Psychologische und logische Untersuchung. Erste Band*
(a) partial transl. by P. T. Geach, in *G&B*. 79–85.
(b) complete transl. by E. W. Kluge, in *Mind*, lxxxi (1972), 321–37.

1895

'Le Nombre entier'
transl. by V. H. Dudman, as 'The Whole Number', in *Mind*, lxxix (1970), 481–6.
'Kritische Beleuchtung einiger Punkte in E. Schröders *Vorlesungen über die Algebra der Logik*'
transl. by P. T. Geach, in *G&B*. 86–106.

1896

Lettera del sig. G. Frege all'Editore, Revista di Matematica
transl. by V. H. Dudman, as 'Letter from Sig. G. Frege to the Editor', in *Southern Journal of Philosophy*, ix (1971), 31–6.

1897

'Über die Begriffsschrift des Herrn Peano und meine eigene'
transl. by V. H. Dudman, as 'On Herr Peano's *Begriffsschrift* and My Own', in *Australasian Journal of Philosophy*, xlvii (1969), 1–14.

1903

'Über die Grundlagen der Geometrie' (Parts I and II)
(a) transl. by M. E. Szabo, in *Phil. Rev.* lxix (1960), 3–17.
(b) transl. by E. W. Kluge, in *On the Foundations of Geometry and Formal Theories of Arithmetic*, New Haven and London, 1971.

1904

'Was ist eine Funktion?'
transl. by P. T. Geach, as 'What is a Function?', in *G&B*. 107–16.

1906

'Über die Grundlagen der Geometrie, I, II, III'.
transl. by E. W. Kluge, in *On the Foundations of Geometry and Formal Theories of Arithmetic*, New Haven and London, 1971.

1912

Anmerkungen zu Philip E. B. Jourdain: 'The Development of the Theories of Mathematical Logic and the Principles of Mathematics: Gottlob Frege' transl. by P. E. B. Jourdain in *QJPAM* xliii (1912), 237–69.

1918/1919

'Der Gedanke. Eine logische Untersuchung'
(a) transl. by A. and M. Quinton, as 'The Thought: a Logical Enquiry', in *Mind*, lxv (1956), 289–311;
   repr. in *Philosophical Logic*, ed. P. F. Strawson, Oxford, 1967;
   and in *Klemke*;
   and in *Logic and Philosophy*, ed. G. Iseminger, New York, 1968.
(b) transl. by P. T. Geach, as 'Thoughts', in *Logical Investigations, Gottlob Frege*, ed. P. T. Geach, Oxford, 1977, pp. 1–30.

'Die Verneinung: Eine logische Untersuchung'
transl. by P. T. Geach, as 'Negation', in *G&B.* 117–36;
repr. in *Logical Investigations, Gottlob Frege*, ed. P. T. Geach, Oxford, 1977, pp. 31–53.

1923

'Logische Untersuchungen. Dritter Teil: Gedankengefüge'
transl. by R. Stoothoff, as 'Compound Thoughts', in *Mind*, lxxii (1963), 1–17;
repr. in *Klemke*, 537–58;
repr. (revised) in *Logical Investigations, Gottlob Frege*, ed. P. T. Geach, Oxford, 1977, pp. 55–77.

INDEX